D1545048

CIRC

FP

911.3 E93
EVERYMAN'S CLASSICAL ATLAS

5.00

INVENTORY 98

INVENTORY 1985

3/6/75

BK 911.3   E93
EVERYMANS CLASSICAL ATLAS

3   C1961   5.00 FP

3000 559609 20019
St. Louis Community College

JUN   CT
of   y

5545 West Park
St. Louis, Missouri 63105

PRINTED IN U.S.A.

Everyman's

CLASSICAL ATLAS

A volume in

EVERYMAN'S REFERENCE LIBRARY

Everyman's Reference Library

DICTIONARY OF QUOTATIONS AND PROVERBS

THESAURUS OF
ENGLISH WORDS AND PHRASES

DICTIONARY OF SHAKESPEARE QUOTATIONS

DICTIONARY OF NON-CLASSICAL MYTHOLOGY

DICTIONARY OF DATES

DICTIONARY OF MUSIC

EVERYMAN'S ENGLISH DICTIONARY

ENGLISH PRONOUNCING DICTIONARY

DICTIONARY OF LITERARY BIOGRAPHY

CONCISE ENCYCLOPAEDIA OF ARCHITECTURE

CLASSICAL DICTIONARY

CLASSICAL ATLAS

ENCYCLOPAEDIA OF GARDENING

CONCISE ENCYCLOPAEDIA OF RUSSIA

DICTIONARY OF PICTORIAL ART (2 volumes)

FRENCH–ENGLISH—ENGLISH–FRENCH DICTIONARY

EVERYMAN'S ENCYCLOPAEDIA (12 volumes)

Other volumes in preparation

Everyman's

CLASSICAL ATLAS

WITH AN ESSAY ON THE DEVELOPMENT OF
ANCIENT GEOGRAPHICAL KNOWLEDGE AND THEORY

by

J. OLIVER THOMSON, O.B.E., M.A.

*Emeritus Professor of Latin at the
University of Birmingham*

LONDON: J. M. DENT & SONS LTD
NEW YORK: E. P. DUTTON & CO. INC.

© Text, J. Oliver Thomson, 1961
All rights reserved
Made in Great Britain
at the
Aldine Press · Letchworth · Herts
for
J. M. DENT & SONS LTD
Aldine House · Bedford Street · London
First published 1961
Second edition 1963

INTRODUCTION TO 1961 EDITION

'THE accompanying Atlas,' says the Introduction to the first edition of *Everyman's Atlas of Ancient and Classical Geography* (1907), 'has been included in this series for the greater convenience of the reader of Grote's *Greece* and other works that ask a continual reference to maps of ancient and classical geography. . . . Among other works which the present Atlas will help to illustrate, editions of Gibbon's *Decline and Fall of the Roman Empire*, and of Merivale's Roman History which leads up to it, are already in preparation; it is hoped to publish in the series also an edition of Herodotus, the father of the recorders of history and geography, who realized almost as well as did Freeman the application of the two records, one to another.' (The promised books duly appeared in Everyman beside Grote's noble array of twelve volumes, and a specially valuable addition was Mommsen's *History of Rome* in four.)

Of the genesis of the Atlas we hear that it 'has the advantage of being the result of the successive labour of many hands. The original author was Dr Samuel Butler, sometime headmaster of Shrewsbury school and afterwards Bishop of Lichfield and Coventry. . . . The work was at a later date twice revised, and its maps were redrawn under the editorship of his son. It has now been again revised and enlarged to meet the special needs of this series.' The Atlas contained no explanatory text but consisted entirely of 27 coloured maps (all folding) and a 93-page index of place-names with their locations by latitude and longitude. And the original price—it is almost unbelievable—was a shilling!

The Introduction of 1952 says that the first Atlas 'has only been laid aside in response to a demand for better maps, clearer in detail.' The second differed in many ways from its ageing namesake. It had a larger page, though only slightly larger, the size being still determined by the format of the Everyman series to which the book was attached. The folding maps were abandoned, and there were then 64 pages of coloured maps, many of them 'double-spreads' (covering opposite pages), which had some obvious drawbacks of their own. The index amounted to 35 pages. In addition there were 15 pages of 'maps and plans of notable battles and districts' and an 'historical gazetteer' of 136 pages giving descriptions of most of these places and a few others, Pompeii having 7 pages, for instance, and Rome as many as 34. This material had its uses, though in default of roomier pages for better maps much of it could hardly compete with the information given in travel-guides and elsewhere.

What was still needed was something to raise the book, if possible, above a mere work of reference, some explanatory text to be followed as a more or less continuous clue. This has now been provided by Professor Thomson's essay on the development of ancient geographical knowledge and theory. There is also a (newly written) section of notes on some battlefields, etc. (with a few sketch-maps): this supplement helps towards the desired continuity, and is also specially concerned to indicate the quality of the historical sources. The coloured maps have been slightly reduced in number, to 56 pages, including 'double-spreads,' which have been retained for the same reason as before. Some of the maps are new, like that of Egypt under the Ptolemies and Romans, pp. 52–3: others have been improved in detail (see the silk routes and the monsoon sailings added on pp. 6–7), and a good deal has been done to relieve overcrowding of names and clear away errors. The index also has been corrected: owing to the maps being rearranged it had to be largely rewritten.

An atlas should contain a fairly comprehensive series of maps and an index of place-names. What else it may contain is nowadays very liberally interpreted, and few are likely to object to our gallery of photographic illustrations.

The traditional title, *Everyman's Atlas of Ancient and Classical Geography*, has been changed in this third edition to *Everyman's Classical Atlas*.

1961.

ANOTHER impression being required, the opportunity has been taken not only to change a photograph but to add considerably to the historical notes, so that this becomes a second edition of the new style *Everyman's Classical Atlas*.

1963.

CONTENTS

CONTENTS

Photographs

THE DEVELOPMENT OF
ANCIENT GEOGRAPHICAL
KNOWLEDGE AND THEORY

AN atlas of ancient geography is expected in the main to serve the student of ancient history by displaying the scenes of the events about which he reads; for this purpose it gives a series of maps correctly drawn in the modern manner but filled with the names of ancient peoples and places. But there is a subject of ancient geography in another and stricter sense, concerned with the question how much the ancients themselves knew of geography, how near they came to modern accuracy in mapping. This belongs to the history of science, of which it is a not unimportant part, though seldom treated so systematically as it deserves. It will help considerably for this kind of geography, and also for history, to attempt here some account of the development of ancient geographical knowledge and theory.[1] The inquiry must follow two lines more or less simultaneously. We must try to ascertain the practical horizon at various periods, that is, how much of the world had become known by the contacts of war, colonization, and trade, and by exploration (if any) for its own sake. We must also ask what attempts were made to map the area thus known and what theories were formed of the earth as a whole.

---

[1] A detailed account with full references to original sources and modern discussions will be found in the writer's *History of Ancient Geography*, Cambridge University Press, 1948.

xiii

1. Very Early Horizons

In the nature of things very little can be conjectured on such matters for the long dim ages before historical record. Evidence from tools and the like suggests drifts of population and wares, but it is too vague for our purpose. The owners of the tools are given clumsy names by archaeologists, but we shall never know what they called themselves or any other peoples within their view, which was probably very limited. As for general ideas, it may be guessed that to them, as to many long after, the sky seemed a bowl covering a flat earth. It is also likely enough that, not being fools, men could already draw on the ground a rough sketch of a journey, as primitive men have been observed to do by modern explorers.

The early civilizations provide information enough to give a fair idea of their horizons, though it leaves gaps and vaguenesses in some directions. The foreign interests of Egypt were mainly in Syria, which she conquered for some centuries in the New Kingdom or Empire (1580–1100 B.C.). The ample records show her in close relations with other great powers, Babylon and Assyria, Mitanni at the Euphrates bend, and the Hittites, encroaching southwards from the plateau of Asia Minor. Europe (not yet so named) is represented by Keftiu bringing gifts or 'tribute' from Crete. About 1200 B.C. the Hittite Empire went down before a great movement of 'Sea-peoples,' including 'Achaeans,' who were barely repelled from Egypt itself. West of the Delta were 'Libyan' and other tribes, but there is no hint of a strait to an outer sea: some blue beads found their way to Britain, but the fact does not prove anything like direct voyages. Southwards trade and arms pushed along the dismal Nubian corridor to the

Sudan. A very early traveller, who brought back a 'dancing dwarf,' need not have gone very far himself, even if this was really a pygmy from the Nile-Congo watershed. The Egyptians never had the curiosity to explore the sources of their own wonderful river. More creditable were their voyages on the Red Sea, notably one depicted on her temple by Queen Hatshepsut (about 1500 B.C.). Ships, still little better than improved Nile-boats, passed with convenient winds down the dangerous coast to Punt or the Frankincense Terraces, generally located beyond the strait, in Somaliland.

The Babylonian records have little to say for distant expeditions. They do not mention ships sailing along the dreary coast to India, but some engraved seals prove contact with the pre-Aryan civilization which has now been unearthed in the Indus valley. The Aryans, entering India by 1500 B.C., seem traceable backwards by Iran to the Caucasus, where they had received some Babylonian wares.

Hittite royal archives of the fourteenth and thirteenth centuries B.C. found near Ankara have revealed much about peoples and languages in Asia Minor, including an official language of Indo-European structure. We hear of Troy in a district of Assuwa, perhaps the original of 'Asia,' and of certain Achaeans encroaching in Cyprus and the south coast.

The oldest civilization on European soil was the Minoan in Crete, so called from a king remembered in Greek legend as the first to rule the sea. The inscribed tablets, those in Linear A, have not yet been read. Quite early Crete seems to have radiated a civilizing influence into the western darkness, to Sicily and Sardinia and perhaps to Spain. The great period of the palaces was 1600–1400; at the end Crete was sacked, probably by Mycenae and other mainland places which had largely borrowed its culture.[1] The Homeric epic, the splendid beginning of European literature, represents them as held by Achaeans and led by an overlord of Mycenae to a war against Troy (about 1200 B.C.), followed by disastrous 'returns.' Soon a wave of ruder Greeks (the Dorians) came down, driving swarms of displaced people to cross the Aegean and bringing on the home-land a dark age from which historic Greece slowly emerged in the eighth century B.C. There is of course the perennial Homeric question: how were these elaborate poems composed and how far do they preserve the tradition of the heroic age? Much discussed from ancient times have been the Catalogues of the Achaeans and of Troy's allies (*Iliad*, ii). And where did Odysseus wander? 'Find the cobbler who sewed the bag of the winds,' said the geographer Eratosthenes, very sensibly: for, whatever may have been really known about western waters, Homer fills them with marvels, and there is not a tangible name beyond Sicily, while his Ocean-stream has nothing to do with a real outer sea. Many have detected in his land of very short nights a rumour drifting down with tin and amber from the north. He knows of the Argonauts as voyaging to Aea, 'the land,' a myth presently to be located by Greek colonists at their farthest east, the end of the Black Sea. His 'noble' and 'just' mare-milking nomads (soon to be named as Scythians) are the first instance of a persistent Greek tendency to idealize the noble savage. By the Ocean-stream he has Ethiopians, the 'Burnt-faces' near sunrise and sunset, and Pygmies, attacked by the cranes which fly south from the Mediterranean winter. He has the name 'Asia' only in the humble form of an 'Asian meadow,' and not yet 'Europe,' which appears soon after, meaning

[1] Their tablets in Linear B, now deciphered by Ventris and Chadwick, prove to be in an antique form of Achaean or Greek.

at first only the north Aegean coast. Phoenician traders appear in Homer as active in Greek waters, but not farther west, though they are later credited with a colony at Cadiz as early as 1100. About 950 they were manning Solomon's ships sailing from the head of the Red Sea to Ophir, which seems from its placing in the Table of the Nations (*Genesis* x) to be not beyond South Arabia.

Very primitive peoples can use sun and stars to tell time or season or direction; they may quite well note the solstices, when the rising or setting sun reaches its most northerly and southerly points, and so on. But from such practical observations it is a long way to science. The Babylonians themselves, who had a good deal of astronomy —though much less in early times than some have thought —were far from attempting any rational theory. For the world as a whole and its beginnings the first explanations were only 'myths' or stories. One widespread in the early civilizations, and found in Polynesia and elsewhere, conceives an original chaos of formless 'waters,' which a god split in two, thus forcing heaven and earth apart. The heaven is an upturned bowl or 'as a tent to dwell in,' and is kept up by a god or mountains or pillars like those 'guarded' by Atlas. The earth is flat (or at best slightly concave) and rests like a plate on the primeval waters out of which it 'appeared'; the Ocean is a circular stream, a sort of horizon. Where does the sun go at night? The attempts to answer are desperate: along an underground Nile, it is said, or behind the high north rim of the earth back to the eastern 'Burnt-faces.'

A few local sketch-maps survive. An Egyptian one on papyrus of about 1300 B.C. shows a mining region in the eastern desert with hills drawn in childish perspective. Babylonia has some plans of towns and of districts, like Nuzi (Kirkuk). It can also produce a general map, a copy of an antique type, with the Euphrates in the centre and the Bitter River or Ocean flowing close around and some 'islands' in triangles beyond, including one 'where the sun is not seen' (text and conception are obscure). Very early ideas are reflected in the Hebrew Scriptures when they talk of 'the circle of the earth' as 'stretched out above the waters,' and of its 'foundations,' expressions which were to cause embarrassment to Christian commentators.

2. THE GREEK HORIZON BEFORE ALEXANDER

Historic Greece emerged in the form of many small city-states on both sides of the Aegean. Those on the Asiatic side developed more quickly, in touch with a Lydian kingdom behind. This obscured their eastern view, till it collapsed (546 B.C.) and they found themselves annexed to a huge Persian empire. Some like the Phocaeans sailed away rather than submit. Swarms of malcontents had left the cities long since to find land and elbow-room elsewhere, and thus many coasts from Spain to the Caucasus had been dotted with colonies (eighth to sixth centuries B.C.). For geography the main result was that the sea, with its Black Sea alcove, was recognized as a lake, except for a strait to 'the sea outside the Pillars called the Atlantic.' Each group of colonies also learnt something of its own hinterland. When the process was nearly over, about 550, Anaximander of Miletus 'first ventured to draw a map of the inhabited earth.' About fifty years later Hecataeus, of the same city, greatly 'improved' the map, and described the earth in two books entitled *Europe* and *Asia*, the latter including Libya (or Africa). This, the first-known general geography, is unfortunately extant only in snippets. Apart from them most of our best matter comes from the history of Herodotus: he wrote (about 440–425) on the epic conflict with Persia, a great subject into which he could bring almost everything learnt on his own travels. We may follow the colonial lines, and sketch what knowledge was acquired in various directions.

Westwards, though the Adriatic was mostly avoided, south Italy became a 'Great Greece.' Important colonies in Sicily were a challenge to Carthage, which protected the western end and warned the Greeks off Sardinia. Cumae, the mother-city of Naples, had to fight the Etruscans, who also drove settlers out of Corsica; the usual ancient view about this people, that they had come by sea from Asia Minor (about 800 B.C.?), is now most often accepted. Finely sited near the Rhône was Massalia (Marseilles), whose wares were soon passing far inland, though Herodotus is ignorant enough to make the Danube rise among the Celts 'at Pyrene' (even later Aristotle can repeat this, except for correcting the supposed town into mountains, the Pyrenees). A few small ports tapped the nearer side of Spain; the outer had been reached early (about 630), when a skipper Colaeus was blown along Africa and out through the strait to Tartessus, then 'a virgin mart,' near Gades. It appears from old matter embedded in the late Latin poem of Avienus that seamen from these places knew the outer coasts to Brittany, and had at least heard of the Hierni (Ireland) and Albion. One Himilco was sent by Carthage to explore on their tracks, and is credited with a vaguely alarming report about sluggish and windless seas filled with monsters; perhaps these were 'Phoenician lies' to deter competitors. Anyhow the Greeks soon began to speak of the Pillars (the Strait of Gibraltar) as impassable, and Herodotus has already become sceptical, unduly so, about nearly everything beyond: while admitting that tin and amber come from the north, he rejects rumours of Tin

Islands or an amber river Eridanus flowing north to a north sea (compare coloured maps 1 and 2).

A chief line of enterprise was towards the Black Sea, politely called Hospitable (Euxine) because it was not. The south coast was quite habitable, indeed, and the tribes behind, if primitive, were not dangerous. Under the Caucasus was Colchis with the river Phasis, sometimes thought the boundary between Asia and Europe. The north coast was bleak in winter, but important for corn and salt fish, hides and slaves. Herodotus, who came here, describes the Scythians without illusions on the noble savage, but his geography is faulty. Remarkable is the account of a route of native traders leading far inland (to the Urals or much farther?): he dismisses as Greek inventions one-eyed Arimaspians fighting gold-guarding Griffins, happy Hyperboreans to the outer sea, and a people said to sleep half the year. At least he knows that the Caspian is a lake and not a gulf of the Ocean, an error which was to revive later to the great damage of the map.

In the south the only group of colonies was about Cyrene; the coast farther west was under the protection of Carthage and poorly known. Egypt was opened through a sort of treaty-port, Naucratis, and many came to see this old and strange land. The greatest wonder seemed the Nile itself, which alone of rivers flooded in the dry season: there was no lack of theories, including the right one of rains on the Ethiopian mountains. Herodotus has a curious report that at the highest point known (beyond Sennar) the Nile flows from the west. He also describes a string of oases at ten days' intervals from Egypt to Ammon (Siwa), Augila and westwards to a Mount Atlas (not apparently the same as his wooded mountains above Carthage) and on to the 'Atlantic Sea.' He has heard a story about some braves of the Nasamones (below Augila): they went inland

and west (south-west?) many days, and were captured by some dwarfish blacks and brought to a town on a big river, which had crocodiles and flowed east (the Niger or only some Saharan wadi?); at Cyrene people understood them to mean the Nile, and Herodotus agrees, as it suits what he heard in Egypt about the Nile coming from the west.

There too he heard something more startling. King Necho (about 600 B.C.), having vainly tried, it was said, to cut a canal between the Red Sea and the Delta, sent his Phoenicians in that sea to sail round the continent. They passed into the southern sea, and in autumn landed wherever they were, and sowed corn and waited to reap it. So in the third year they reached home through the straits. No detail is given but one: they declared that when rounding Libya they had the sun on the right. Herodotus rejects this but not the voyage itself. 'Thus was the extent of Libya first discovered.' A tremendous feat indeed, and it is hard to believe that it could have been done at all, or done with so little effect on the development of geography. Many, however, have believed precisely because of the sun detail.[1] Herodotus himself knows so little of the 'extent of Libya' that he denies any inhabited land south of Arabia!

A Persian noble, Sataspes, ordered to carry out the same task, started from Morocco; after going south many months to some dwarfish people, who fled from their 'towns' to the hills whenever he landed, he came back to report that he had 'stuck' (in the Guinea current?), and he was disbelieved and executed. Herodotus knows too that Carthaginians sailed down that coast and did a dumb barter for gold. We have a translation of an inscription set up at Carthage by Hanno, telling how he planted seven colonies along Morocco and beyond to Cerne; from this

[1] So recently Franz Hampl in *Gnomon*, 1950, pp. 352–4, who dismisses my doubts in *H.A.G.*, pp. 71–2.

base he made reconnaissances to a big river Chretes and to another with crocodiles and hippopotami, and past forests and fires (bush-burnings?) and a high mountain to an island with wild men, called by the interpreters Gorillas, of whom three were taken and flayed. The document has omissions and obscurities, but it is generally agreed that Hanno reached Sierra Leone at least (some take him to Cameroon in eruption). Garbled reports were soon current, and the gain for geography was less than it should have been, the coast being even misread as running south-east instead of south-west. As for the islands, very likely the Carthaginians visited the Canaries and perhaps Madeira.

Eastward the horizon was filled by a huge Persian empire, which had absorbed several older civilizations. By supporting a revolt of her Ionian kinsmen Greece drew on herself formidable invasions, which were gloriously repelled. Herodotus, who had travelled to Babylon, displays his knowledge in a long catalogue of provinces and another of 61 peoples represented in the Persian army, also an account of the imperial road 93 days from the Aegean to the capital Susa. His geography is often faulty even for this nearer half of the empire, still more for Iran, though he can name a remarkable series of peoples as far as the Sacae beyond Bactria. He knows of India, the Indus valley, as added by Darius, who sent a Greek in his service, Scylax, down the river (wrongly supposed to flow east): a few things are said about the peoples, strange birds and beasts and plants, and the tribute paid in gold-dust, very queerly obtained. From the Indus the same officer, we hear, sailed in thirty months to the head of the Arabian Gulf, thus proving the existence all along of 'the southern sea called the Red' (our Indian Ocean). Yet Herodotus has a poor idea of this coast, and can tell about Arabia little but fables.

In the interval between Herodotus and Alexander a little more geography was learnt. Greek mercenaries of a rebel Persian prince marched to near Babylon and had to retreat northwards, cutting their way through a maze of snowy mountains to the Black Sea. Their story is told by one of their elected leaders, Xenophon (see coloured map 10 and sketch-map 4). Another Greek, Ctesias, was a doctor at the Persian court, and said some new things about India, with a taste for monstrous peoples and strange animals, including unicorns. Outer Europe remained poorly known: Aristotle could still make the Danube come from the Pyrenees, though he had a good idea of rivers flowing north from Arkynian mountains (the later 'Hercynian Forest' in south Germany—the name is Celtic and means 'oak'). Plato used the blank of western waters for his own purposes, to conjure up and sink an immense Utopia, Atlantis, larger than Africa plus Asia (as then known), with lesser islands and a continent beyond. For the description he naturally used local colour from varous sources, and the sinking accounted plausibly for alleged shoals in the outer sea.

3. GREEK THEORY TO ARISTOTLE

Hitherto people had not asked questions about causes, or had answered them only with myths. About 600 there began in Ionia a new kind of 'wise men': very boldly, if one considers the slender basis of observation and experiment, they asked what was the ultimate 'nature' (*physis*), which changed into other things. Thales, still influenced by the myth of Ocean, pronounced this substance to be water, and the earth a slab floating on the primal water. Anaximander began with a sort of chaos, out of which things were defined; already he had the earth, in the form of a pillar-drum, swinging free in the middle of the universe. Anaximenes took a step back: the earth, he thought, is a thin slab resting like a lid on the primal air, and the sun goes sideways round, screened at night by the high northern parts (another early idea is that the earth, which was once in the plane of the sun, has got a southward tilt out of that plane). For all the Ionians the surface of the earth is what it seems, a flat (or slightly concave) disk. On such a disk Anaximander drew the first general map of the inhabited earth, a map presently improved by Hecataeus. Herodotus, echoed by Aristotle, laughs at those who draw the earth as perfectly round and girdled by the Ocean-stream, a statement hardly fair, as the name Ocean was now transferred to real outer seas, and the known earth lay well within the conventional round frame. There was already a central length-line foreshadowing the later Gibraltar-Rhodes parallel. Greece and Ionia, lying midway between the sunrises, it was said, have the best-tempered climate, and are the natural home of free men. Herodotus regards an outer sea as not proven except between the Indus and Gibraltar. He has a curious notion of a symmetry between the Danube, flowing east and south, and the Nile, flowing east and north, their mouths being 'opposite' (on the same meridian). For these early ideas in mapping see maps I and 2, with the frame of the Ionian map.

The theory of climatic influence is carried far in an essay *On Airs, Waters, and Sites* ascribed to the doctor Hippocrates; between a cold and wet northern plain and a hot and dry southern plain is a middle belt with diversity of seasons and of soil and landscape: only here are the people both strong and intelligent. Such ideas were to be still more discussed when the earth was understood to be a globe. It is fair to the Ionians to add that they made many acute observations on kindred matters like earthquakes and volcanoes, the silting action of rivers, and fossil shells, which, found in places far inland, prove old sea-floors; these remarks were to be often repeated later, with only minor elaborations.

Pythagoras, who settled and founded his fraternity in the toe of Italy about 530 B.C., left no writings, and soon became a legendary figure. If he himself thought of the earth as a globe, it seems likely that he kept it at the centre of the universe, an improvement on Anaximander's drum. But he is nebulous already for Aristotle, who prefers to speak of 'the Pythagoreans' or 'mathematicians' in general, and complains of their arbitrary and mystical reasoning. They were not interested in the primal substance, he explains, but in the forms of things, and thought the whole heaven a harmony: as ten is the 'perfect' number, the celestial bodies must be ten, the heaven of fixed stars, the five planets, the sun, the moon, the earth and a counter-earth (invented to make up the number): they must be 'perfect' spheres, revolving in 'perfect' harmonious circles. Round what? A central fire, for fire is 'worthiest' to occupy that place of honour. We never see this fire, because our face of the globe is turned away from it, and we never see the counter-earth, because the central fire lies between. Elsewhere this system is ascribed specially to Philolaus (about 425). Certainly it was Plato who gave wider currency to the idea of the earth as a globe. In one of his imaginative 'myths,' put in the mouth of Socrates, he conceives the earth as hanging unsupported in the middle of the universe; it is a globe so huge that the known inhabited earth of the Mediterranean basin is only a niche in its surface (*Phaedo*, 108d–111c). His later myth about Atlantis is inconsistent in detail with this fancy, but still implies an enormous globe. Plato set the problem, we hear, how to 'save the appearances' while keeping the regular circular movements round a stationary earth. Eudoxus of Cnidus (about 370 B.C.) answered with an ingenious system of twenty-six concentric spheres moving round differently orientated axes. Perhaps his was the earliest known figure for the circumference of the globe, 400,000 stades, accepted rather casually from 'the mathematicians' by Aristotle. Eudoxus may have observed that the star Canopus, just above the horizon at his own Cnidus, rises high in Egypt: the marked difference in so short a distance proved that the earth must have a pronounced curvature and therefore be very small relatively to the universe. The figure, however, is not nearly small enough. By now the globe was being 'divided into zones after the analogy of the heaven-sphere,' though there were still no good data for placing the tropic on the actual map, much less the arctic circle. Eudoxus thought the length of the known earth twice its breadth, and seems meant by Aristotle to be among 'the mathematicians' who leave a comparatively narrow Ocean from Spain westwards to India (some remarks on this suggestion were not without echoes down the ages to Columbus).

Aristotle did an immense work in organizing the sciences now emerging more distinctly from the general background of philosophy. He accepts the earth as a globe, with at least two reasons from observation (the round shadow on the moon at eclipses, and the change in the stars as one travels north or south). But he will have it that the earth has a 'natural place,' resting at the centre of the universe. The upper world is filled with a fifth element having a 'natural' circular movement, another notion not healthy for science. He left no formal treatise on geography, but touched on the subject chiefly in the *Meteorology*; this deals with the world of change below the moon and the combinations of the four elements which go on there.

4. THE HELLENISTIC AGE AND ITS SCIENCE

It was Philip of Macedon who imposed union on Greece. His son Alexander led the great *revanche* against Persia; in a few dazzling years (334–323) he marched to the Indus and back to die at Babylon. Much of his vast conquests was retained under dynasties founded by his officers, the Ptolemies and Seleucids, and they were still prosperous when the shadow of Rome began to fall their way, about 200. This was the heyday of the Hellenistic age, when Greek civilization was spread widely among peoples hitherto thought 'barbarian.' The triumphant march brought, of course, a great increase of direct and detailed knowledge, especially for the farther parts like India. Several of Alexander's companions left good accounts, and these are reasonably fully preserved through writers who copied them. The gains for geography were well used by Dicaearchus, a pupil of Aristotle, and above all by Eratosthenes, who was librarian of Alexandria about 234–196 B.C. He could base his mapping on his own remarkable measurement of the globe. The gist of his book can be fairly well recovered from Strabo, who used it freely along with the criticisms of Hipparchus.

The conquest of Iran involved very long detours all over the country to Bactria and the river Oxus and the Jaxartes (Syr-daria), where a 'Farthest Alexandria' was founded (Khojend). Later a kingdom set up by Greek governors in Bactria had a stirring life, with adventures deep into India; it was at once isolated by a native Parthian kingdom which placed itself astride the main road east of the 'Caspian Gates' (about 250). Very strangely, just when better knowledge might have been expected, imperfect exploration (by one Patrocles) encouraged a wrong notion of the Caspian as a gulf of the outer Ocean.

In India, after being halted by his mutinous men on the Beas, Alexander moved slowly downstream. At least two companions and later Megasthenes, a Seleucid envoy at Palibothra (Patna), wrote interesting descriptions: they have mistakes and exaggerations of course, including wild rumours of monstrous tribes in remote parts. Something was known of the geography beyond the Indus valley, a royal road 10,000 stades on to Patna, past which the Ganges continued 6,000 stades eastward (the final south-ward bend was not realized). The great 'Snowy' range (Emodus, Imaus) was supposed to run not south-east but due east to the eastern Ocean. Taprobane or Ceylon was heard of surprisingly early.

From the Indus Alexander marched west with heavy loss through the sand-dunes of Baluchistan, trying to keep in touch with the fleet sent off under Nearchus. We have the latter's detailed report of the voyage along the coast of wretched Fish-eaters and then up the east side of the Persian Gulf. On his return to Babylon Alexander dispatched officers to explore the west side, and one rounded the great south cape, but Arabian waters were still un-familiar, and room could be found there for a new Utopia, the Panchaean island of Euhemerus (300 B.C.).

When it came to mapping the new data, there were great difficulties. Dicaearchus had the idea of continuing the great central parallel of Gibraltar–Rhodes eastwards through the Caspian Gates and along the base of the Indian mountains; on the whole this line is remarkably correct. Eratosthenes adopted it, and drew another (very rough) parallel from Ethiopia to south India, arguing from the similarity of their climates, their plants and animals, and their black peoples. Between the two parallels thus obtained he fitted in the reported Indian distances, at the cost of twisting the peninsula to point south-east. The

Indus was supposed to flow south and overestimated, so that its mouths were pulled far below the tropic, and with them the Fish-eater coast and most of the Persian Gulf. In this way the mapping worked along from India, and many mistakes were made with the second 'section,' Ariana or Iran, and so on westwards (see coloured map 3).

Perhaps Alexander might have had the Nile completely explored and Africa sailed round. The Ptolemies did nothing so heroic. For a time they needed war-elephants, and sent officers to Adulis (near Massawa) and other ports thereabouts to organize hunts inland. The unalluring coast was minutely known all the way to the Cinnamon Country and the Cape of Aromata or Perfumes (Guardafui). The cape was barely rounded, and the rest of the outer coast of Africa was a guess, the stretch explored by Hanno being still misdrawn as running south-east. Several travellers went far up the Nile, and described strange tribes and customs: the source-lake of the Blue Nile was known, and the rains long assumed to cause the Nile's flood were now attested. The Nile was very important for the mapping of Eratosthenes and his measurement of the globe.

Alexander did not live to do much in the west, where he might have attacked Carthage and perhaps Rome. These barbarian powers now came to the forefront, fighting each other about Sicily and then in a mortal struggle, in which Hannibal marched from Spain and over the Alps into Italy, but had to return to be defeated near Carthage. The Greeks still had surprisingly hazy ideas of northern geography, with some old fancies like a Danube branch to the Adriatic. But a remarkable voyage was now made by Pytheas of Massalia, about 320. Very regrettably we have only scraps about him, chiefly from writers who thought him an arrant liar. He can be followed, rather vaguely, to

c

Brittany and round Britain, and to an island with amber off the Elbe (hardly the Prussian amber coast, as has sometimes been thought). He said striking things about Thule, northmost of the British Isles, six days north of Britain and near (apparently one day from) the Frozen or Curdled Sea: we hear that the barbarians pointed out where the sun went to sleep for three or two hours. Recently Thule has been most commonly understood as central Norway rather than Iceland, and as actually reached by him.[1] He had scientific interest enough to measure the shadow at Marseilles very well, and to take sun-heights at various points on his voyage, and he was apparently the first to connect tides with the moon. His report of habitable lands lying far north was accepted by Eratosthenes, but later rejected by many, to the great damage of the map (they had some excuse, as no one had any suspicion of the Gulf Stream or its modifying influence on the climate).

We hear from the great mathematician Archimedes of somebody (Dicaearchus?) making a new estimate of the globe, a shorter and better one, as 300,000 stades. It has been credited also to Aristarchus of Samos, who died about 230. This ancient Copernicus came to the true theory that the earth, while rotating about its own axis, revolves round the sun. But he made it revolve in a circle, instead of an ellipse; so he failed to 'save the appearances,' and his hypothesis won hardly any support at the time or later. Eratosthenes made a brilliant estimate of the globe. He worked with sundials at two places, Aswan (Syene, S on the diagram) and Alexandria (A), supposed to be on the same meridian, as the Nile flows almost due north. At Syene at the summer solstice at noon the sun's ray R falls straight on the gnomon or pointer G and makes no shadow. At the same time at Alexandria the ray r (parallel to R)

[1] See Hampl, loc. cit., against my doubts in *H.A.G.*, pp. 147–50.

makes with the pointer g a shadow which is $\frac{1}{50}$ of the circle of the bowl. Now the pointers continued downwards would meet in the centre of the earth C; the angle ACS = Aga, and AS must be $\frac{1}{50}$ of the circumference of the earth (the fraction is very near the truth). For the ground distance between the places he adopted a figure of 5,000 stades. The required circumference was therefore 50× 5,000 or 250,000 stades, and he raised it, we are told, to

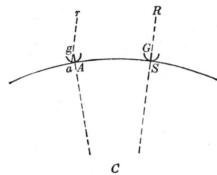

Figure 1. *How Eratosthenes measured the earth-globe*

252,000, to be divisible into units of 60 (rather than into 360 degrees, a notation apparently first used by Hipparchus). He was aware of various chances of error, and in fact Aswan is 37 miles north of the tropic and 3° east of Alexandria. But he checked with observations at the winter solstice and found the arc the same as before. The method is brilliant, on the assumption that the earth is a perfect globe (he could not suspect that it is flattened at the poles). How good is the result? The stade was usually read as 8⅓ or roughly 8 to the Roman mile, but many good authorities think he used a very short stade of 157·5 metres. If so, the total works out very near the truth, less than 200 miles short; with more ordinary stades it is some 12–14° in excess. On the globe thus measured he proceeded to fit the known earth by calculating its breadth and length along two great lines intersecting at Rhodes.

The breadth extends from the Somali coast—for the 'torrid' zone is habitable so far south—to Thule near the arctic circle. The length, plotted along the great central parallel, works out as 70,800 stades from Cape St Vincent to the Ganges mouth, or, with allowances for the projection of India and possible islands, 78,000 stades. Thus the known earth occupies only about two-fifths of the way round the globe on that parallel. What of the unknown remainder? If one could sail west from Spain, would there be a clear sea to India or some 'perioikoi' or 'dwellers round' on the way? Perhaps he thought rather of clear sea, but he was not given to speculation about the unexplored.

All this good work in geography was far from being common knowledge, and the current philosophies treated science as quite subordinate to ethics. The Epicureans valued science as a weapon against superstition, but had little insight for what was really science, so that they laughed at Antipodes and denied the globe itself; the Stoics at least accepted these things, and their leaning to astrology was not quite unfavourable to good sense in geography.

5. THE ROMAN CONQUEST AND CONTEMPORARY SCIENCE

The Roman Republic was now launched on a career of conquest resulting in the mastery of an *orbis terrarum* round the inner sea. The process sometimes threw light on parts hitherto poorly described by the Greeks, as in the northern hinterland. In the east it was at best a case of taking over some relics of Alexander's heritage; the scenes were novel to the Romans themselves, but their campaigns added little to general knowledge, unless about corners like Armenia and the Caucasus. For exploration beyond the range of their arms they did nothing as yet, though an occasional new report came, like the first ill-understood rumours of the Silkmen or Chinese. Polybius, the chief historian of the times, who knew the Romans well, asked himself how these exceptional barbarians had subjected 'almost all the inhabited world' in half a century, and other writers sometimes talked naïvely as if their dominions included 'all lands not inaccessible.'

In the east Pompey penetrated to the Caucasus and within three days of the Caspian, which was generally assumed to be a gulf. It was he who set the stage for the long feud with the Parthian empire across the Euphrates. Caesar meant to conquer it, and Antony got as far as the Tabriz region, but had to retreat. Isolated by Parthia were the Greek kings of Bactria, who now invaded India well beyond Alexander's limits, but thereby exhausted their own kingdom, so that it was overrun by nomads from the east. These last are also mentioned by the Chinese Annals: we hear how Yue-chi at the west end of the Great Wall were driven west by the Hiung-nu or Huns, and how a brave envoy, Chang K'ien, regained contact with the fugitives when they were conquering Bactria (128 B.C.), whereupon his master cleared the western roads past the Tarim oases and sent caravans over the roof of Asia. Now too there are mentions from the western side of the Seres and their silk (*sericum*). (For these remote parts see map 24).

By the Red Sea the Ptolemies traded with Sabaean middlemen in Aden, but about 120 B.C. an adventurer, Eudoxus of Cyzicus, with the help of an Indian pilot saved from a wreck, sailed twice to India (perhaps still only coasting?). When Egypt was at last annexed in 30 B.C., there was a boom in sailings to India with the handy monsoon winds. Mere romancing is the far-eastern Utopia of Iambulus.

From the northern seaboard of Africa campaigning and exploration did not go deep, and the accounts of the hinterland and the west coast show little improvement. There is a remarkable story about the Eudoxus just mentioned. On his way back from a second voyage to India he was blown down East Africa and found the figurehead of a ship, which, it was thought, must have come from Cadiz round the continent; he also took down some native words. Later he started from Cadiz himself and reached a people speaking the same language. On another attempt he was apparently lost, a lame conclusion which suggests that the story is not altogether untrue. Whatever he did, it had no effect on geography: there was still no idea of the enormous size of Africa, and some were not sure that the sea did continue all the way round.

Europe itself was now much better known. Spain, nearly all occupied as two provinces, is well enough described, though some could still make the Pyrenees run north to south. A province in south Gaul was just in time to save Italy from a great German migration, the first recorded, that of the Cimbri and Teutoni. The rest of Gaul was conquered (58–50) by Julius Caesar, who repelled a German king and chose the Rhine as the frontier; his work was destined to be more lasting and important than Alexander's. His adventures to Britain, 'almost another world,' caused a sensation, and his own account has interesting features; presently Strabo, in his dislike of Pytheas, ruined the mapping, and dubious things were still repeated about Tin Islands. Caesar made two raids against the Germans, who retired into their 'solitudes and forests.' From Macedonia the Republic fumbled towards a Danube frontier, and Caesar meant to deal with the formidable Dacians beyond the river. Northern parts were still not well known, and some could believe a wild story about Indians driven past the Caspian 'gulf' to Germany.

A curious development of theory was due to Crates (about 165 B.C.), who wrote on Homer and explained Odysseus as wandering in outer seas. He had a fancy of four symmetrical land-masses on the globe, separated by equatorial and interpolar Oceans: besides our inhabited earth there are 'dwellers round,' 'dwellers opposite,' and Antipodes. The idea had a certain fascination, and was often repeated later. For progress in geography the task was to criticize the work of Eratosthenes, and this was done by the great astronomer Hipparchus, who observed in 161–126. He attacked the procedure in detail, showing that the mapping involved impossible triangles, and he rightly insisted on the need of a better groundwork of observations: he could add some latitudes from Pytheas, but even he could not supply useful longitudes, and his criticism, as reported by Strabo, often sounds rather perverse. The historian Polybius liked a practical kind of geography more to the taste of his noble Roman friends, and made the mistake of rejecting Pytheas, as did Artemidorus. The Stoic Posidonius studied tides at Cadiz, and had much to say of the universe and the 'sympathy' of its parts. Being mainly concerned to show the smallness of the earth in the universe, he made a new and not very respectable measurement[1] from the difference of the height of Canopus at Rhodes and at Alexandria: he got 180,000 stades, which, on any ordinary stade, is much too little. He made the length of the known world go half way round on the parallel of Rhodes, leaving an unexplored half (of

[1] See p. xliv below on Ptolemy and my *H.A.G.*, pp. 212–13.

clear sea?) from Spain west to India. He had an idea, like
Polybius, that the equator was not 'torrid' but actually
less hot than the tropics. The Romans ignored this improvement, and held by the usual five zones, only two of
them habitable. They were at best parvenus in science,
and the national poet admits that it was not their *métier*
(he himself makes some blunders about the zones). Cicero
in an admired passage, the *Dream of Scipio*, uses the fancy
of Crates (see the orb of Crates inset with map 5).

6. THE ROMAN EMPIRE AND THE OUTER WORLD

The Empire as established by Augustus in 27 B.C.
enjoyed two centuries of peace almost unbroken, at least
within its frontiers. Town-life and civilization spread;
travel was safe, and there was much mingling of races.
The Empire was something more than a 'ring of lands'
round the inner sea, and its writers, impressed by its size,
often talked as if there were nothing outside it, or only a
barbarian fringe not worth the taking. For a practical
people, the Romans did little exploration, but some
traders went beyond the wall of the legions, and others
sailed with the monsoon winds to India: a little was heard
by land and sea even of China.

For geography we have the large-scale work of Strabo,
who outlived Augustus: it is written for general readers
and concerned far more with description than theory. The
astronomer Ptolemy, about A.D. 150, makes an elaborate
effort (after Marinus) to map the knowledge of the time.
The first extant work in Latin, by Mela (A.D. 43), is a bad
attempt to show how he can write up an intractable
subject. Pliny's grandiose encyclopaedia (A.D. 79) has a
mass of information, good and bad: the relevant books
(iii–vi) are overcrowded with rigmaroles of place-names.

North Europe was now better known. Augustus tried hard for an Elbe frontier, but after a reverse fell back on the Rhine-Danube. Later there was only a slight advance to an outer line in South Germany. A remarkable essay by Tacitus describes the Germans eastward to the amber coast, with very primitive Fenni beyond; he knows of Suiones (in Sweden), but has not Pliny's Scandinavia or Ptolemy's comparatively small island of Scandia. Ptolemy's map of Germany (with 69 tribes and 95 'towns'!) has all sorts of mistakes in drawing and details. Britain was now conquered (A.D. 43 on). Tacitus wrote a life of Agricola, governor in 78–84, who pushed north to fight the Caledonians, while his fleet 'had a glimpse of' Thule (here meaning Shetland); there is talk of a 'sluggish sea' hereabouts and also beyond the Suiones, where the last gleam of sunset continues to the dawn. Ptolemy's map is surprisingly detailed and reasonably well shaped, though Scotland is twisted round to get it in south of Thule. Even Ireland, which was never in the Empire, has a fair number of names.

The Danube frontier was mainly the work of Augustus. Trajan added a huge outer bulwark by conquering Dacia (101–7), and Marcus Aurelius had hard wars beyond the upper river (167–80). From the mouths Roman influence reached along to the Crimea. Little was known of what is now Russia, and Ptolemy's outline is bad, though he has the Rha (Volga) flowing to the Caspian, rightly made a lake again. The Tanais (Don) was usually thought the boundary between Europe and Asia.

The old province of 'Africa,' a useful granary, was easily defended by holding the Aurès range, which was finally opened up to the Sahara. Westward a client kingdom under Juba was soon annexed, and there were two provinces of Mauretania, Caesariensis and Tingitana.

There was little Romanizing inland, and no formal frontier towards the desert. One notable expedition penetrated over the high Atlas to the Wadi Ghir. Little was done for the exploration of the outer coast, on which old fables are repeated. Ptolemy makes it run south-south-east till after Hanno's last names it fades into unknown land. He draws his first meridian through the Happy Isles (the Canaries), wrongly placed only $7\frac{1}{2}°$ west of that of Gibraltar.

From Tripolis there was an early campaign deep inland to Garama in Fezzan. We have tantalizingly brief notices of two men who travelled far into the Sahara, three months south from the Garamantes, it is said, or four months to Agisymba, a rhinoceros country with Ethiopians. Ptolemy, slicing the exaggerated figures of Marinus, still gets $16\frac{1}{4}°$ south, which is certainly much too far: some have thought of Asben or Tibesti, others more probably of the Lake Chad region about $14°$ north. King Juba, reviving an old notion, made the Nile flow from a lake in Mauretania with crocodiles, and under the desert to a Lake Nigris, and so east and north. Quite different is Ptolemy's conception of two sprawling river systems, the Nigeir and Geir, with a watershed range between and neither connected with the Nile. There are not, and never were, such rivers, but his drawing was to be often repeated and to influence speculation on the unknown interior until about 1825.

Up the Nile there was a campaign against the Ethiopians, and Nero sent scouts much farther to vast swamps choked with vegetation, no doubt the sudd barrier about $9°$ north. There was trade down the Red Sea with a kingdom of Axum (in Abyssinia). The coast is described past Guardafui to the Zanzibar region and some way on (Ptolemy reckons to $16\frac{1}{4}°$ south). From these parts came hearsay of Nile lakes, and Ptolemy drew two with headwaters draining from Mountains of the Moon, a happy guess (not without some rumour of the Ruwenzori?). At the end he made the coast turn east to become the southern shore of a closed Indian Ocean; this *terra australis* was to cause great trouble till it was disproved in a long series of voyages from Vasco da Gama to Captain Cook.

In the East wars with Parthia continued, the frontier being unsatisfactory, especially about Armenia. At moments Roman arms reached the Persian Gulf, and Trajan, watching a ship leaving for India, sighed for Alexander's youth. Iran usually appears as a vague background, but Ptolemy has (from Marinus) a remarkable notice of one Maes, a Syrian merchant, who sent his agents to Bactria and beyond to tap the silk trade from China. From the Chinese Annals it is known that an able general, Pan Ch'ao, had reopened the Tarim silk-roads, and sent an envoy to Babylonia, who picked up a vague notion of Ta-ts'in (the Roman Empire, especially Syria). Modern explorers of the silk-roads like Sir Aurel Stein have found much evidence of a strange mingling of influences, including a classical Athena on an Indian seal east of Khotan. The agents knew Stone Tower (Daraut-kurgan?) near 'the starting-point of traders for Sera the capital' (Irkeshtam, where the Alai trough leads to Kashgar?). Sera is no doubt Si-an, near the bend of the Yellow River. The final journey to it was said to be seven months. Marinus, counting this as if continuous and due east, got Sera at 228°; Ptolemy after drastic reductions gets $177\frac{1}{4}°$. (On the silk routes see map 7).

There was a swift development of monsoon sailing from Egypt to India (Augustus even made a surprising aggression on Southern Arabia to clear the way). At first ships went to the Indus and Barygaza (near Surat), but presently they took a diagonal cut across to Malabar. We hear plenty on the wares, chiefly spices, and complaints of the drain of bullion to pay for such things. The *Periplus of the*

Red Sea, perhaps about A.D. 50, is detailed on the west coast of India. Ceylon was still strangely exaggerated, and the east side of India poorly described, though quite early Italian pottery has now been found at an 'Indo-Roman trading station' close to Pondicherry. Ptolemy's map of India has an amazing number of names, but somehow he has utterly misconceived the run of the coasts and almost flattened out the peninsula.

The *Periplus* knows that ships sail from East India to Chryse ('the Golden'), and beyond Chryse and well to the north the sea ends in a country with a great city Thina, from which silk is carried overland to Bactria; this is the first notion of China as approached by sea. According to the Chinese Annals 'envoys' (really traders?) from Tats'in came to the Tongking frontier in 166. Ptolemy can name at least one skipper, Alexander, who went far east on the tracks of Indian traders and colonists. His mapping, difficult to interpret, goes past the Golden Chersonese or Peninsula to the Sinae with a capital Thinae behind its port of Cattigara; this last is usually put somewhere near or in China, and recently gold medallions of the Antonines have been found in Cochin-China. But whereas the *Periplus* is right on the general run of the coast, Ptolemy pulls it down to merge into a *terra australis* enclosing the Indian Ocean.

7. CONTEMPORARY THEORY

The main writers have been cited in the previous section, but more must be said on theory. Strabo's work deserves credit for its large design, but he has little taste for the theoretical side. He accepts the measurement of Eratosthenes without explaining the method. He spoils the map of Europe by rejecting Pytheas. He reckons the known

world as 70,000 stades long and thinks that in the unknown remainder from Spain west to India there may be
at least another inhabited world. For mapping he is content for his purposes with lines crossing at right angles. He
has a good deal of interest in matters of physical geography. Mela dismisses the globe and its zones in a few
paragraphs. Pliny explains fairly correctly about these
things, though not without a certain undertone of naïve
awe at the cleverness of the Greeks in measuring the earth
and inventing Antipodes who do not fall off. The moralist
Seneca writes with considerable interest and competence
on *Natural Questions*. In arguing that the globe is tiny
relatively to the universe he remarks that the distance
from Spain west to India is only a very few days with a
fair wind; elsewhere he foretells that the Ocean will reveal
'new worlds' and Thule will not always be the farthest
known land (both sayings were echoed down the centuries
to have their effect on Columbus). The Stoic poet Manilius,
an enthusiast for astrology, has very intelligent views of
the earth-globe and its climates. Various others have good
remarks on these matters, though Tacitus betrays a
startling ignorance in trying to explain the short northern
nights. A verse primer of geography by Dionysius Periegetes is of no value for science.

Maps are not very often mentioned, but often enough to
show common use for military and other purposes: many
senators must have had even maps of the Empire without
being suspect of dangerous thoughts and put to death,
like one under Domitian. There is a late story of an imperial survey by four Greeks for Julius Caesar and
Augustus. Anyhow the latter, completing the work of
Agrippa, set up a map of the Empire in a public portico;
it showed a very Roman reliance on road-measurements,
but need not have been a mere diagram of the road-system

like the later Peutinger map. More important for science was a *Correction of the Map* by Marinus of Tyre, known to us only through Ptolemy. He had the merit of using the latest reports to extend the map far east and south, but got extravagant results, because, as Ptolemy says, he did not allow nearly enough for the exaggeration of travellers, and their halts and divergences. He had a very rough sort of projection with meridians drawn at right angles through degree points spaced in due proportion along one important parallel (Ptolemy permits this only for the provincial maps, as making no material difference within small areas).

As an astronomer, Ptolemy was interested only in the task of mapping, not in description. Already in his *System* (the Almagest of the Arabs) he had explained how to put the known earth on the globe, half the way round in the north temperate zone and overlapping southward into the 'torrid'; also how 'climates' are determined by their longest day and by shadows, with an elaborate series of such latitudes up to the arctic circle. In the *Geography*, or rather *Instruction in Map-drawing*, he insists that mapping should be based on astronomically fixed points, though few latitudes were available.

The body of the book is a list of 8,000 places, each with its co-ordinates of longitude and latitude; it all looks formidably scientific, but the vast majority are merely reckoned from itinerary distances. From the figures readers can draw maps for themselves, a laborious process (whether he helped them further by publishing his own maps has been questioned). Apart from a world-map, there can be drawn either a set of 26 land-groups, as he recommends, or another of 63 smaller regions including, for instance, four provinces in Gaul.

Unhappily he (and Marinus) adopted for the globe the

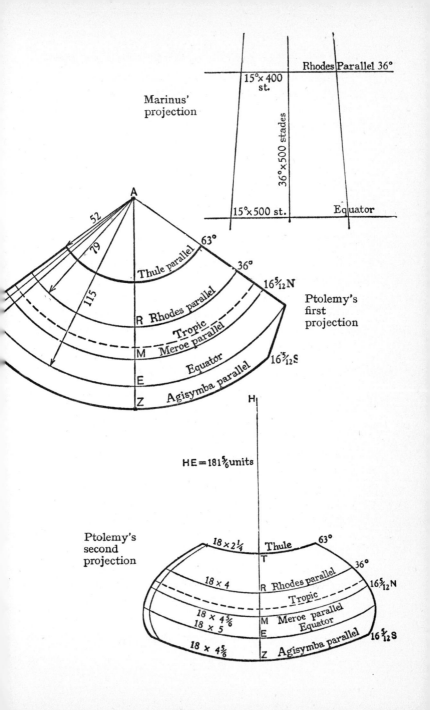

Marinus' projection

Rhodes Parallel 36°

15° × 400 st.

36° × 500 stades

15° × 500 st.

Equator

A

52

79

115

63°

Thule parallel

36°

Ptolemy's first projection

16 5/12 N

R Rhodes parallel

Tropic

M Meroe parallel

Equator

E

16 5/12 S

Z Agisymba parallel

H

HE = 181 5/6 units

Ptolemy's second projection

18 × 2 1/4

Thule

63°

T

18 × 4

R Rhodes parallel

36°

Tropic

16 5/12 N

18 × 4 5/6

M Meroe parallel

18 × 5

Equator

E

18 × 4 5/6

z Agisymba parallel

16 5/12 S

bad figure of 180,000 stades,[1] and so a degree of 500 stades, or 400 on the parallel of Rhodes. With this false gradation the Mediterranean is badly exaggerated as 62°, and the error accumulates eastwards. For reasons mentioned above he reduces the figures of Marinus, at first moderately to Stone Tower, then by half for the final stretch to Sera, but still gets 177° (instead of 228°), and he confirms this by calculations for the sea-route to Cattigara. Yet the total distance is only 126° on the modern map (to Si-an). The lengthening of Asia on a too small globe was of course to encourage Columbus. (For these eastern calculations of Ptolemy see map 5.)

For the scientific map Ptolemy suggests two projections, as follows. The first has curved parallels to be drawn from A with radii of the length indicated: then along the Rhodes parallel space out 18 meridian points 4 units apart westwards and as many eastwards. It is a simple conical projection with one standard parallel, the meridians south of the equator being slanted back.

The other shows both the parallels and the meridians (except one) as curved. The radii are from H, and the same number of meridians is drawn as before spread 4 units apart on the parallel of Rhodes (they will be $2\frac{1}{4}$ apart on that of Thule). The improvement is obvious, though there is increasing distortion the farther we go from the central meridian.

8. The Decline

With the decline of the Empire came times of anxious defence and disastrous invasion, when a widening of the geographical horizon could hardly be expected. Trade

[1] Some defend him as meaning this in terms of a long 'royal' stade of 210 metres. See p. xxxv above on Posidonius.

narrowed its range, and the outer lands receded from view. A few new things were learnt about the various barbarians who flung themselves on the frontiers, some coming from far like the Huns. But the writers are apt to repeat stale matter about Scythians and other old peoples instead.

The Germans attacking over the Rhine were Franks and Alemanni, new leagues formed from old tribes. The Goths moved south from the Vistula, and Dacia was abandoned to them (271); they became dangerous again a century later, when pushed by the Huns. A flood of Sueves and Vandals and others burst over the western provinces in 407. In 476 the last feeble western Caesar was deposed by his German king-maker. The eastern Empire had its own bad neighbours, Slavs and Bulgars and Avars, and Justinian (526–65) should have repelled them and not wasted his strength in recovering parts of the west. In his time some new things are said about the original home of the Goths in the Scandinavian 'island,' described as Thule or Scandza. Britain was long raided by northern Picts, Scots from Ireland, and Saxon pirates, before being abandoned in 410 and fading for a while into a haze of fable.

For Africa we find little but echoes of old reports. There is a minute seaman's guide to the Libyan coast. Towards the end Cosmas has fresh matter about Axum and 'the mouth of the sea which they call Zingium' (the sea of Zenj, as 'Zanzibar' means). Most assumed a continuous sea round Africa, ignoring Ptolemy's idea of unknown land.

In the east there were wars with Persian kings, who had replaced the Parthian. Sometimes they are mentioned as turning away to deal with enemies appearing in their rear. Strangely almost all the writers revert to the obstinate error of a Caspian 'gulf.' They do not actually state that the Huns came from farther east than the Caspian steppes,

D

but the Chinese Annals seem to connect them with the old Hiung-nu (and also the Avars with a people driven from Mongolia by the Western Turks, about 552). There is still evidence of a silk trade and the consequent overlapping of cultures in Central Asia. The Chinese Annals have a few new things about Ta-ts'in, though the hearsay is little better than before. For western writers India became for long a hazy Utopia. At last (about 547) there is a fresh report comparable with the old *Periplus*. The monk Cosmas, once a trader in the Indian Ocean, names with their wares ten ports in Western India down to the Pepper Coast of Male, and two more round the corner. He knows of local churches. Ceylon (Sielediba) is still absurdly over-estimated, but is real enough as forwarding to the west sandalwood, cloves, and silk from regions as far as the silk country of Tzinista, plainly China with a Persian form of the name. The Persians were now controlling the supply of silk by sea and overland, but soon certain monks from 'Serinda' (Khotan?) explained to Justinian that silk was made by worms, and brought him some eggs, so that henceforth silk could be produced in Roman territory.

A few of the writers are transcribers of Ptolemy like Marcianus. More important, because commonly read in the Middle Ages, were copiers of Pliny such as Solinus and Martianus Capella (about 400?), who at least deserves some credit for keeping alive the idea of the globe and Anti-podes. The Middle Ages also liked a geographical chapter in Orosius. Two versifiers, Avienus and Priscian, thought it worth while to translate the verse primer of Dionysius Periegetes. A lowly kind of geography is that of the road-books, which do not bother about the earth being a globe. We have a comprehensive *Itinerarium Provinciarum Antonini Augusti*, giving roads with stations and distances as far as the frontiers: possibly much of the matter was

transcribed from a copy of a general map drawn under
an Antonine, Caracalla (211–17). There are itineraries
written by and for Christian pilgrims to Jerusalem as by
one of Bordeaux about 333 and by Aetheria about 395.

We hear a little of maps. Campaigning maps are mentioned as *itineraria picta*. Under a church in Moab was
found part of a mosaic map of the Holy Land (about 550).
The Gallic orator Eumenius in 297 pleads for a map of the
world to be displayed in his native place (Autun), evidently
thinking of Agrippa's. The Peutinger world-map at Vienna
is apparently a thirteenth-century copy of something far
older. The form is peculiar, a parchment roll over 21 feet
long by only a foot wide. As a map this ribbon is absurd,
but its aim is only to give roads with their stations, so that
seas and roadless lands are narrowed to a mere indication.
K. Miller tried to fix the original as of 365 and by one
Castorius cited by the Geographer of Ravenna (about
670). But, if some Christian features are set aside as later
additions, the ultimate source may be a copy of the road-
map of Caracalla's time mentioned above.

Despite such 'practical' maps, many had right ideas
about the globe and its zones, though the 'torrid' was
again taken too literally. Astrologers like Firmicus
Maternus were not the least intelligent in these matters
(Ptolemy himself had defended astrology). Very popular
in the Middle Ages was the commentary of Macrobius
(about 400) on Cicero's *Dream of Scipio*, with its fancy
(deriving from Crates) of four symmetrical land-masses on
the globe. A translation by Chalcidius of Plato's *Timaeus*,
with the Atlantis story, helped to keep alive the notion of
a western continent.

The decline of science had set in before the Christians
became strong, but they helped its demise. Some were
ready, if the Scriptures left the case open, to adopt the

usual pagan science. But the earth of the texts was obviously a flat disk, established above the waters, and the Fathers took every line but the right one of admitting that these expressions were not revealed truth but old Jewish notions as obsolete as Homer's. There was an increasing reluctance to avow the globe, and special reasons were produced against Antipodes. Lactantius already scoffed at these and denied the globe. So we come again to Cosmas with his *Christian Topography*, written to show that the pagans were all wrong and the Antipodes an old wives' tale: the sun is quite small and disappears nightly behind a huge conical mountain in the north: after the pattern of the tabernacle of Moses the inhabited earth is an oblong with an Ocean round it, and beyond this an outer earth where men dwelt before Noah. Thus by strange paths geography has returned to its Ionian beginnings, and even behind them to crude eastern fancies. But despite such vagaries the best of the ancient achievement in this science was remembered and passed on.

NOTES ON SOME BATTLEFIELDS, ETC.

THE Ionian Greeks on the coast of Asia Minor suddenly found themselves annexed to a huge empire of the Medes and Persians developing in their rear (546 B.C.). A belated revolt was crushed, Miletus being sacked (499–494). Only two homeland cities, Eretria (in Euboea) and Athens, had sent a little help, but it was enough to draw invasion on Greece and bring on the supreme crisis of her fate (the great Persian war of 490 and 480–479 B.C.). The primary source is the history of Herodotus, written about 430 B.C., one of the most charming and interesting of books (English commentaries by R. W. Macan, 1895, 1908, How and Wells, 1912: translations by A. D. Godley, Loeb, 1921–6, G. Rawlinson, Everyman series, and A. de Sélincourt, Penguin, 1954. The account is of course not always credible about numbers, and leaves other doubts and obscurities. What really happened in ancient battles, as in modern, is often not easy to ascertain: the militarily minded will find more or less discussion in the regular histories, and there is even an atlas of ancient battles full of rival interpretations (Kromayer and Veith, *Schlachtenatlas zur antiken Kriegsgeschichte*, 1922–8). Two recent comprehensive studies by A. R Burn, *Persia and the Greeks: the Defence of the West, 546–478* B.C., and C. Hignett, *Xerxes' Invasion of Greece.*

MARATHON. In 490 B.C. King Darius sent an expedition straight across by the Aegean islands to chastise the offending cities; with it went the exiled Athenian tyrant Hippias. Eretria was soon betrayed and carried away captive, and Hippias guided the enemy over the strait to the bay of Marathon, about 26 miles north-east of Athens. The full levy of Athens marched, some 9,000 or 10,000 heavy infantry, and was joined by 1,000 from an old friend, Plataea; an urgent appeal by runner reached the Spartans 'on the very next day,' but they insisted on waiting five days till the full moon and started too late to take any active part. Modern conjectures tend to put the Persian numbers not vastly higher than the Greek. Miltiades, placed in effective command by a generous casting vote, charged down about a mile, it is said,

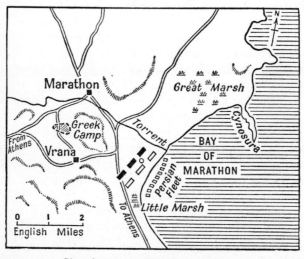

Sketch-map 1. *Marathon*, 490 B.C.

towards the beach; his deep wings broke through the enemy's and then closed round the centre and drove it to the ships, though only a few ships were taken. Herodotus gives the casualties as about 6,400 Persians and 192 Athenians. It seems that the Persian plan had been to lure the Athenian army to Marathon and keep it there until a force landed to seize Athens in collusion with some partisans of Hippias inside. The signal was to be the flashing of a shield on Mount Pentelicus, and it duly flashed, but Miltiades too saw it and marched back in time, so that the

Persians arriving off Phalerum could only sail away
(Herodotus, Bk vi. 102–17; Grote, *History of Greece*,
vol. v. 43–73 in Everyman ed.; J. A. R. Munro in *Cambridge Ancient History*, vol. iv, ch. 8).

THERMOPYLAE AND ARTEMISIUM, 480 B.C. (Herodotus, vii. 172–viii. 23; Grote, vol. v, ch. 40; Munro in
C.A.H. iv, ch. 9; much of Herodotus in M. I. Finley, *The
Greek Historians*, 1959). Darius could not forget his check
at Marathon, but the inevitable invasion of Greece was
delayed because he died in 486 and his son Xerxes had
first to reconquer Egypt. At last in 480 the vast preparations were complete, including a bridge of boats over the
Hellespont and even a canal cut through the peninsula of
Mount Athos, where a large Persian fleet had been
wrecked in 492. The figures given by Herodotus for the
enemy's sea and land forces are admittedly fabulous
(J. B. Bury, *History of Greece*, 3rd ed., revised by R.
Meiggs, 1951, suggests as reasonable perhaps 800 triremes
and 300,000 men, while Munro reduces much further still).
It was truly the Athenians, says Herodotus, who were the
saviours of Greece: next to the Gods they repelled the
invader, standing firm against gloomy oracles from Delphi
(vii. 139). It was their Themistocles who had built their
navy up to 200 ships, two-thirds of the allied fleet, and
yet did not press their claims to the command, as the
allies would serve only under Sparta.

The first plan was to send 10,000 men to hold the
entrance into Greece by the pass of Tempe under Mount
Olympus, but on hearing that Xerxes might use a more
inland pass the leaders hastily retreated, and the Thessalians, left in the lurch, naturally submitted to the
enemy. The next line of defence was the pass of Thermopylae, while the fleet could fight hard from a good base at

Artemisium and prevent any landing in the rear of the pass (map 20). On the whole the sea-fighting was indecisive, though the Persians suffered heavy losses from storms, as when they sent a fleet round outside Euboea to turn the pass. Sparta, once again delayed by a holy day, sent ahead King Leonidas with a royal escort of 300 Spartiates; he picked up Peloponnesian and other levies and occupied the pass with perhaps some 7,000 men or more. For two days he repelled frontal attacks until a traitor guided the enemy round by a mountain path to come down in his rear. Before the last stand most of the contingents were allowed to march away: 1,100 stayed with the Spartans. On the news of the glorious disaster the fleet withdrew down the Euripus and round to Salamis.

The landscape at Thermopylae has been so completely altered by the silt of the river Sperchius that a pass of about 14 yards between cliff and sea has been widened into a marshy plain of 1½–3 miles.

SALAMIS, 23 September 480 B.C. (Herodotus, viii. 42–97; Aeschylus, *Persae*, 377–480; Grote, vol. v, ch. 41; Munro in *C.A.H.* ix. 304–14). Soon the army and fleet of Xerxes arrived in Attica, and he had the satisfaction of burning Athens, though almost all the population had been evacuated. The Spartans and other Peloponnesians thought now only of withdrawing to build a wall across the Isthmus of Corinth. To induce them to stay Themistocles had to threaten to sail away with his 180 ships to find a new home at Siris in Italy. He also sent a secret message to Xerxes that the Greek fleet meant to escape under cover of darkness. Thus he forced a battle in the narrow eastern channel of Salamis, near the islet of Psyttaleia, where numbers were not an advantage, and

the Greeks won a brilliant victory under the eyes of the
King enthroned on the hill of Aegaleos (map 20). 'Be
sure,' said Themistocles, 'we have not done this by our
own might. It is the work of Gods and Heroes, who were
jealous that one man should be King at once of Europe
and of Asia' (Herodotus, viii. 109). But a great effort was
still needed for the deliverance of Greece. Xerxes fled back
to Asia in fear for his bridge, but he left Mardonius to
winter in Thessaly with a large and picked army, though
not probably 300,000 men.

PLATAEA, 479 B.C. (Herodotus, ix. 15–70; Grote, vol.
v, ch. 42; Munro in *C.A.H.* iv, ch. 10), In the spring
Athens on refusing tempting offers by Mardonius was again
occupied and again sacked. He then retired to a position
behind the Asopus covering his base at Thebes and with
open ground suiting his numerous and excellent cavalry.
At last after so many selfish hesitations and heroic half-
measures Sparta acted promptly under the regent Pausanias, nephew of Leonidas. He summoned a full levy of the
Peloponnese, and it was joined by 5,000 Athenians and
other contingents of Central Greece till it became a real
national army (110,000, says Herodotus, ix. 28–9; Munro
accepts about 80,000). Coming down the northern foot-
hills of Mount Cithaeron, Pausanias repulsed a cavalry raid
and was encouraged to try a flanking movement towards
the Plataea–Thebes road. But, galled by cavalry attacks
and anxious for water and supplies, he ordered a night
retreat, which was ill executed, the centre column going
much too far. At dawn Mardonius hurried in eager dis-
order to the attack. In the end Pausanias chose his moment
well, and, with his Spartans and Arcadians at first bearing
the brunt, 'won a victory the most glorious of any known
to us.' The enemy camp was stormed and Mardonius

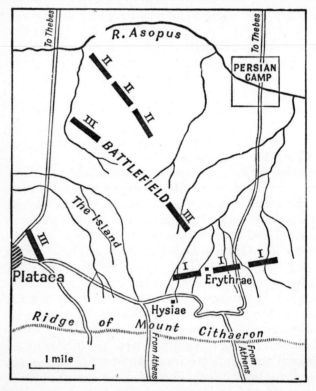

Sketch-map 2. *Plataea. Three Greek positions before the battle*

killed with all but 3,000 of his men, it is said; his base at Thebes was taken, and its 'Medizing' traitors executed.

MYCALE. On or about the day of Plataea came an important victory by sea. A Greek, mostly Athenian, fleet, sent to create a diversion in Asiatic waters, found a large fleet beached beside an army at Cape Mycale near Miletus, and burned both ships and camp. While the

Spartans now slacked off, Athenian generals continued
the work of liberation, taking the lead in organizing the
Confederacy of Delos, which began almost at once to
turn into an Athenian naval empire. The chief crusader
against Persia was Cimon, son of Miltiades, who won
south Asia Minor for the Confederacy by a brilliant victory
at the river Eurymedon (467). Later, when he was in
exile, a fleet crossed from Cyprus to help a rebel prince in
Egypt, though it came to disaster, together with a relief
squadron (449–454 B.C.). Presently, when Cimon died in a
successful campaign off Cyprus, Pericles made an informal
peace with Persia.

The western colonies took practically no direct part in
the defence against Persia, but some had formidable
'barbarian' enemies nearer home. An exiled Sicilian
tyrant invited Hamilcar of Carthage, who came with
300,000 men, it is said, and was overthrown at Himera by
Gelo, the brilliant tyrant of Syracuse. This was in 480
B.C., if not 'on the very day of Salamis' (Herodotus,
vii. 166), and there is no doubt that Carthage was in
concert with Xerxes. Gelo's brother Hiero helped the old
colony of Cumae to beat the Etruscans (474).

Resentment against the naval empire of Athens brought
about the Peloponnesian War (431–421 and 413–404 B.C.).
It is described (down to 411) by a supremely great historian,
Thucydides (translations by B. Jowett, C. F. Smith in
Loeb ed., R. Crawley, parts in Finley, *Greek Historians*).
In the first phase Pericles turned Athens into an island,
immune from any decisive blow by land. Later she was
terribly weakened by the Sicilian adventure, and Sparta
accepted Persian subsidies to build for command of the
sea and cut the Black Sea corn-supply: much of the
fighting was therefore in the Hellespont region, including
the final disaster at Aegospotami. (On the war Adcock in

C.A.H. v, ch. 8; Ferguson, ibid., ch. 9–12; Grote is very full and elaborate, vols. vi–viii in Everyman ed.)

SPHACTERIA. A notable early incident of the war was that of Sphacteria (Thucydides, iv. 2–6, 8–23, 26–41; Adcock in *C.A.H.* v. 230–5). In 425 an Athenian fleet under Eurymedon, reconnoitring towards Corcyra (Corfu) and Sicily, was wind-bound at the peninsula of Pylos in Messenia, just north of the barren island of Sphacteria which shelters the bay of Pylos (or Navarino). He kept his men occupied by building a fort, and, when he went on, he left Demosthenes with five ships to hold it. The Spartans summoned forces to blockade it and landed 420 hoplites (with attendant Helots) on the island. Eurymedon, turning back to relieve his colleague, entered the bay and drove the Spartan fleet ashore, thus cutting off the island garrison. Sparta offered to send envoys to treat for peace. Pericles would have accepted, but he had died in the plague of 429, and the new-style demagogue Cleon refused. Hostilities dragged on, the garrison being fed by feats of blockade-running. Feeling turned against Cleon, who blamed the generals and boasted that he would have easily finished the business if he had been in command. Nicias thereupon resigned in his favour, and the people took both men at their word. Cleon was at first disconcerted, but promised to liquidate the garrison in twenty days with only a modest non-citizen force. 'Crazy as his promise was, he fulfilled it.' Nearly 300 surviving hoplites were captured, about 120 of them full Spartans, a shock to the prevailing belief that Spartans never surrendered.

The Bay of Navarino was to see the defeat of an Egyptian and Turkish fleet by a British, French, and Russian under Sir Edward Codrington in 1827, an event which ensured the independence of modern Greece.

Sketch-map 3. *Siege of Syracuse*, 414–413 B.C.

SYRACUSE. In 415 B.C. the Athenian democracy voted
a splendid armada of 100 triremes, which presently became
134 with allied ships, to further its interests in Sicily (some
dreamed of conquering the whole island and even of
challenging Carthage). Of the three generals Nicias thought

some minor display of power enough, while Lamachus wanted to sail straight against Syracuse; the 'middle view' of Alcibiades prevailed, though he was early recalled and fled to Sparta, where he did his country deadly harm by his advice to send an able officer, Gylippus, to organize the defence of Syracuse. In 414 Nicias landed north-west of that city and seized the plateau of Epipolae behind; he quickly pushed his siege-walls southwards over the plateau and down to the Great Harbour, despite counter-walls and the death of Lamachus. Unfortunately some northern gap let Gylippus in at a critical moment, and he transformed the situation: by a counter-wall (S 4) he practically raised the siege on the land side. Soon he was taking the offensive in the Great Harbour also. On the appeal of Nicias, Athens in 413 sent another fine armada of 73 ships under Demosthenes and Eurymedon. The former, repulsed with heavy loss from S 4, advised instant retreat by land, but the superstitious Nicias delayed starting owing to an eclipse of the moon. Thucydides describes with great power the battles in the Great Harbour and the agonizing retreat of over 40,000 men, till the last surviving prisoners perished in the quarries of Syracuse (much of vi and vii given by Finley, *Greek Historians*).

XENOPHON. The 'anabasis' or 'march up country,' after which Xenophon names his book, really ended when Cyrus was killed at Cunaxa in 401 (*Anab.* i. 8. 27). Presently, when their generals were treacherously seized and murdered at the Great Zab (ii. 6. 1) and when they had elected new ones, including Xenophon (iii. 1. 47), the Greeks began their resolute retreat northwards towards the Black Sea. It is described in Books iii and iv, and the climax is the thrilling moment on Mount Theches when all started running at the sight of the sea (iv. 7. 24).

Sketch-map 4. *Expedition of Cyrus*, 401–399 B.C.

The march through Armenia is still variously drawn, see especially the *Schlachtenatlas*, which gives Belck's line, approved by Lehmann-Haupt, but also discusses several rival routes. Translation by R. Warner, Penguin.

Issus. October 333 B.C. (Arrian, *Anabasis Alexandri*, ii. 6–11: translation by E. J. Robson, Loeb; A. de Sélincourt, Penguin, 1958. See Tarn, *C.A.H.* vi, ch. 12.) Alexander, having subdued Asia Minor (or as much of it as he needed to meanwhile), was expected in Syria, but was delayed at Tarsus by a chill caught by bathing in the river Cydnus. At last he moved down the coast road by Issus to Myriandrus, past a site marked for an Alexandria and still bearing his name today as Alexandretta or Iskenderun. Hereabouts the road turned inland to the Syrian Gates (the Bailan Pass). He understood Darius III to be at Sochi, eastward of the pass in open country well suited for his numerous cavalry. But Darius, apparently misreading his delay as due to hesitation or fear, had gone round behind Mount Amanus and so down to Issus, where he massacred the sick left in a camp. He was now posted in Alexander's rear in the narrow plain of a steep-banked river, the Pinarus, no doubt the Deli Tschai. After a moment of incredulity Alexander turned back eagerly to accept battle. The ancient numbers for the Persians are wildly exaggerated. It was probably only after his victory here that Alexander definitely formed the design of conquering the whole Persian Empire (his father Philip had thought at most of Asia Minor).

Alexander did not pursue Darius eastwards but moved south to seize his naval bases, the Phoenician ports. This task was completed by the storming of Tyre after one of the most extraordinary of ancient sieges (Jan–Aug. 332: Arrian, ii. 18–24). Egypt submitted easily. In 331 Alexander came back through Syria to cross the Euphrates at Thapsacus. He did not go down that river but turned east through 'Mesopotamia,' where the heat was less fierce and fodder easy. Darius had had ample time to assemble a new

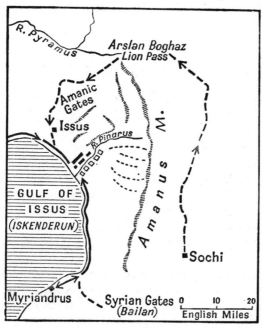

Sketch-map 5. *Battle of Issus*

imperial army, and awaited him at Gaugamela, on the Bumodus, a tributary of the Lycus or Great Zab, some 18 miles north-east from Nineveh and Mosul (it was 60 from Arbela, after which the battle was often named because Alexander pressed the pursuit thus far). Here was a plain suited to cavalry (there were also scythed chariots and some elephants). Alexander is given about 47,000 men.

E

The Persian army list and battle order have many echoes of Herodotus with their distant peoples, and Arrian repeats talk of a million foot and 40,000 horse and of 300,000 Persian casualties. The natural prizes of this crowning victory were Babylon and Susa (1 Oct. 331: Arrian, iii. 7–15).

THE CAUDINE FORKS. For centuries a chief interest of the history of Rome is the slow but sure conquest of Italy. It was sure because she had a political prudence which Athens and Sparta never had, and knew how to extend the privileges of her citizenship. The tradition of the chroniclers is retold in Livy's splendid narrative (Everyman translation, vol. ii; Mommsen, *History of Rome*, Everyman ed., vol. i, pp. 338–79; Adcock in *C.A.H.* vii, ch. 18). It contains duplications of victories and other falsifications from patriotic and family pride. The 'First Samnite War' is suspect as a fiction to justify Rome's dealings with the Campanians in the Latin revolt. In the 'second' or great Samnite war of 327–304, and a 'third' or final in 298–290, the combatants were not perhaps so conscious or far-sighted as Mommsen represents. A notable early incident was the trapping of both consular armies in a hill-pass, the Caudine Forks, on the track of the future Appian Road between Capua and Beneventum (321 B.C.: Livy, Bk. ix. 2–11). The Samnite general C. Pontius disarmed and released them in return for hostages and a pledge to observe the terms; the Roman Senate refused to honour this as a treaty and tried to hand over the consuls and others as scapegoats, though it was not unnaturally suggested that it would be more honest to replace the armies in the pass. Beneventum was as yet called Maleventum, itself a pun on a Greek name meaning Appletown: it was changed to 'well come' when a colony was founded in 268. In 275 Pyrrhus of Epirus, a kinsman of Alexander, was finally defeated here, after two 'Pyrrhic' victories over the Romans, and driven from Italy. An Alexander of Epirus had already come and been killed in Lucania in 331. Livy is inspired to a picturesque digression on what would have happened if Alexander the Great had lived to meet Roman generals like Papirius Cursor, the avenger of the Caudine Forks (ix. 17–19; for Pyrrhus see Frank in *C.A.H.* vii, ch. 20). By the second century B.C. Rome had become niggardly in diffusing her privileges, and the Italians had to extort them by the Social War (91–89 B.C.); it was the Samnites again who fought most bitterly.

PUNIC WARS. (Mommsen, vol. ii, Everyman.) It was inevitable that Rome and Carthage should quarrel about Sicily: geographically it is Italian. The First Punic War, 264–241, was fought mostly in and round Sicily (T. Frank in *C.A.H.* vii, ch. 21). At sea the Romans had everything to learn, and they learnt fairly soon and well to fight the lumbering sea-battles of the time, but the losses from storms were so enormous that the disheartened Senate gave up building, and it was a fleet built by public subscription that won the final victory. After a big sea-battle at Cape Ecnomus in 256 there was a first Roman invasion of Africa; it was good policy, as Carthage's Libyan subjects were always ready to revolt, but it was mismanaged. Sicily became the first 'province.' Soon afterwards Sardinia and Corsica were grabbed to deny their use to Punic fleets. Hamilcar sought to compensate the loss of Sicily by building (or rebuilding) an empire in Spain: his son Hannibal, who had been sworn as a boy to vengeance, provoked the Second Punic War, 218–201 (Mommsen, ibid.; Hallward in *C.A.H.* viii, ch. 2–4).

Hannibal had 59,000 men at the Rhône, we hear, and

descended into Italy with 26,000. The losses seem very heavy, but he had bad luck in stiff resistance from the mountaineers and in the late season. (In 207 his brother Hasdrubal brought a large army across apparently without serious difficulty and by the same pass, Livy thought, though another question started about this.) The problem of Hannibal's pass, and indeed his whole line from the Rhône, is insoluble on the evidence (Polybius, iii. 50–6; Livy, xxi. 31–8). Polybius has not a single name between the Allobroges and the Insubres, one which suggests a wide detour by the Little St Bernard in the Graian Alps; Mommsen, op. cit. ii. 96–103, argued confidently for this (after Wickham and Cramer). Livy is irreconcilable with Polybius, having contaminated him with some secondary source. Most agreed, he says, that Hannibal descended first among the Taurini. Recent writers have therefore inclined to some pass nearly west of Turin, the Cenis (or a local variant, the Clapier), or the much-used Genèvre in the Cottian Alps. The story of Hannibal's showing his men a prospect of the Italian plain below may of course be dismissed as rhetoric. A case by Sir Gavin de Beer, *Alps and Elephants*, 1955, for a southern line and an obscure southern pass, the Traversette, is demolished by F. W. Walbank in *Journal of Roman Studies*, 1956, 37–45.

Hannibal had hoped to rouse the Cisalpine Gauls, then in process of conquest by Rome, which had just founded colonies at Cremona and Placentia. Many thousands did begin to join him after his victories at the Ticinus and the Trebia. In the spring of 217 he crossed the Apennines into Etruria, probably by the Collina pass, and ambushed the consul Flaminius in a narrow defile along the north shore of Lake Trasimene (Polybius, iii. 82–5; Livy xxii. 3–7; Hallward in *C.A.H.* viii. 43–8). In 216 the Senate, bored with the tactics of Fabius 'the Delayer,' decided to give

Hannibal his pitched battle in the Apulian plain at Cannae, with something like 86,000 men against his 52,000 (Polybius, iii. 107–18; Livy, xxii. 43–9; Mommsen, op. cit. ii. 119–22; *C.A.H.* viii. 52–5). The battle was complicated, with a brilliant co-ordination of infantry and cavalry tactics. It was the blackest day in Roman history, and the Italian federation was seriously shaken, but even now he could not take Rome. He was never properly reinforced, and his last chance vanished in 207, when his brother Hasdrubal, who had slipped past Scipio in Spain and crossed the Alps, was intercepted and destroyed at the Metaurus in Umbria, after a famous march by the consul Nero from Apulia, 250 miles in a week, to join his colleague in the north (Polybius, xi. 1–3; Livy, xxvii. 46–9; *C.A.H.* viii. 93). Presently Scipio's invasion of Africa from Sicily brought about Hannibal's recall and his final defeat at Zama (or rather Naraggara) in October 202. Philip V of Macedon had resented some Roman police-work against Illyrian pirates; he had allied himself with Hannibal after Cannae and had 4,000 men at Zama, facts which were to have serious consequences for his country. In 197 he was easily defeated with his phalanx at Cynoscephalae in Thessaly, and ordered to keep his hands off Greece; his son Perseus was overthrown in 168 at Pydna in his own kingdom and deposed; in the same year a terrible example was made of Epirus, 150,000 people being sold into slavery. In 146 Corinth was razed with the same excuse, and after a short Third Punic War Carthage was brutally destroyed (Mommsen, op. cit. iii. 22–38; Hallward in *C.A.H.* viii, ch. 15; in an epilogue Charlesworth finds it 'hard to name anything which mankind can be said to owe to Carthage').

Spain, which had been so dangerous in the hands of Carthaginian generals, was kept as two provinces, Hither and Farther, Spain (197 B.C.) The conquest of the

'Celtiberian' tribes was slow and not without disgraceful reverses. A native hero was the Lusitanian (Portuguese) guerrilla leader Viriathus (154–138). In the Roman civil war Sertorius became popular in Spain (80–72 B.C.) and did much to hasten its Romanization.

When the Romans had landed in Africa (206), one Numidian king had joined them against the other. He was rewarded with a huge kingdom from Mauretania to Cyrenaica and the task of goading Carthage into a last desperate war, after which her small territory became a province of 'Africa' (146). A bastard prince, Jugurtha, played hard for the kingdom, bribing or defying the increasingly corrupt and incompetent Roman Senate (112–106 B.C.).

THE ROMAN REPUBLIC AND THE EAST. While philhellene Roman generals were freeing the Greeks, not always anxious to be freed, from the Macedonians, the Seleucid king Antiochus III, still a Grand Monarque, was advancing northward in Asia Minor and even over the straits into Europe. But the Romans stopped him dead at Thermopylae, and easily beat him back to overthrow him at Magnesia in Lydia: they forbade him to encroach north of the Taurus (190 B.C., see map 24). They were still slow to annex, but the appetite for easy spoil grew, and when their friend Attalus, King of Pergamum, bequeathed his kingdom (133 B.C.) they suppressed a native rising and set up a province of 'Asia,' the prey of greedy governors and tax-farmers. (Roman Asia included most of the fertile western seaboard of Asia Minor: map 54 does not represent political divisions at one historical moment.) No other province was taken till Cilicia in 103, as a base against pirates and useful for intervention in Cappadocia behind 'Asia.' Rome was distracted by civil

strife, and Mithridates of Pontus could make a long effort
to drive her out, with his ally Tigranes of Armenia, who
had extended his kingdom towards Syria at the expense
of the last feeble Seleucids. A terrible incident of the first
Mithridatic war was a wholesale massacre of Roman
citizens in the Greek cities of Asia (88 B.C.). The third war
began with another bequest of a kingdom, Bithynia in
75. An able general, Lucullus (74–66), overran Pontus and
Armenia till his army mutinied and he had to wait to
hand it over to Pompey. Before Pompey the kings could
only retreat, Mithridates finally to the Crimea: Tigranes
was allowed to keep Armenia proper, without his
additions. Pompey turned south to Syria, which he
treated as vacant and annexed (64). He did not annex
very readily, relying on client-princes like a king in
Galatia, a High Priest of the Jews, various Arab sheikhs and
others. It had been 92 when a Roman general (Sulla)
made the first diplomatic contact with Parthia: Lucullus
made a threatening gesture, and Pompey refused to
recognize a Euphrates frontier. Crassus came seeking a
military fame to balance Pompey's and was overthrown
at Carrhae (Harran) in the Mesopotamian desert, Syria
itself being very nearly lost. Caesar no doubt meant to
avenge the disgrace. Antony penetrated far east to
Media Atropatene, but was obliged to retreat, and a
persistent and embarrassing question of prestige was left
to the emperors. Augustus was content with a diplomatic
victory, enforcing the return of the standards of Crassus
(20 B.C.).

A First German Wandering. Of great interest
as foreshadowing things to come is the first historical
movement of German people, at a time when the name
German, as distinct from Gaul or Celt, had barely been

heard of. The migrants were the Cimbri and Teutoni of Jutland and near by (Mommsen, op. cit. iii. 167–83; H. Last in *C.A.H.* ix. 139–51). After a clash with a consul in Austria the Cimbri, taking some Celtic Helvetii with them, moved into south Gaul, where the Romans had formed a small province of Narbonensis, with colonies at Aquae Sextiae (Aix) and Narbo. A consul was defeated, another killed, another with a proconsul beaten with enormous loss at Arausio (Orange). Fortunately the Cimbri turned into Spain and out of it again, while the Teutoni roved in Gaul, and Marius had time to prepare. He overthrew the Teutoni with tremendous carnage at Aix on the way to Italy, and turned back to take the main part in destroying the Cimbri at Vercellae after they had come down through the Brenner (102–101 B.C.).

THE CONQUEST OF GAUL, 58–50 B.C. (Caesar's own *Commentarii de Bello Gallico*, i–vii; Mommsen, op. cit. iv. 196–271; C. Hignett in *C.A.H.* ix. 537–73; C. Julian, *Hist. de la Gaule*, ii–iii. 1920–1, etc.). Caesar's work was of decisive importance for western civilization. He saved Gaul from the Germans in his time and gave it several centuries of peace in which to become so Romanized that it could absorb the great barbarian invasions. As a feat of military skill and energy his achievement far exceeded Pompey's settlement of the eastern provinces; he conquered a great and warlike people, though this was possible only because it was weakened by faction and intertribal jealousies.

He began by forcing back the Helvetii, moving again under German pressure. He beat an encroaching German king in Alsace and proclaimed the Rhine as the Roman frontier (later he found time for two short deterrent raids across the river, in 55 and 53). To warn the Britons off helping their Gallic kinsmen he risked a reconnaissance to Britain in 55 and something more ambitious in 54 (T. R. Holmes, *Ancient Britain and the Invasions of Julius Caesar*, 1907). A strong Belgic confederacy gave some hard fighting, especially the Nervii. Of special interest is the struggle of the Veneti of Brittany with their stout oaken ships. In 52 a widespread revolt found a national leader in Vercingetorix of the Arverni (Auvergne). He had a scorched-earth policy but relented to spare Avaricum of the Bituriges (Bourges). Caesar stormed it but was repulsed from Gergovia, and even old friends like the Aedui rose. Vercingetorix now drew Caesar southwards to defend the old Province (Narbonensis), but, failing in an attack, retired into Alesia. Caesar besieged it and was himself besieged by a Gallic relief army (250,000, he says). After two repulses this huge levy dispersed; Alesia was taken and little was left to deal with but local risings.

Caesar could be only too Roman in his cruelty, and he mentions with hardly a tremor his wholesale slaughters and enslavements (e.g. iii. 16. 4, *itaque omni senatu necato reliquos sul corona vendidit*).

CAESAR'S GAMBLE. When he crossed the Rubicon in January 49 B.C. Caesar's first aim was a pitched battle in Italy, but the 'Caesariana celeritas' defeated its own end and Pompey got clear away from Brindisi in March. From now Caesar took enormous risks. He did not follow Pompey east but decided to deal first with his officers in Hither Spain: after some luck and some reverses he forced their surrender at Ilerda (Lerida), and Varro in the Further province easily submitted, so that all Spain was subdued in forty days (Caesar, *de Bello Civili*, i. 37–87; Mommsen, op. cit. iv. 360–5; Adcock in *C.A.H.* ix. 648–51). In the first days of 48 he crossed the Adriatic

despite the enemy'e fleet, and later Antony's legions got
over to join him only with luck. At Petra (near Dyrrhachium, Durazzo) he showed an impudent rashness: with
a half-starved army, strung out over fifteen miles, he
besieged one twice as strong. After a break-through by
Pompey he could only disengage himself and retreat
towards Thessaly, with his fortunes in ruin (Caesar, op.
cit. iii. 31–74; Mommsen, iv. 380–6; *C.A.H.* ix. 654–62).
For Pompey the way back to Italy lay open; but he
unwisely chose to follow Caesar and give him the pitched
battle he wanted, near Pharsalus (Caesar, op. cit. iii.
75–99; Mommsen, iv. 386–92; *C.A.H.* ix. 662–6; Scullard,
From the Gracchi to Nero, 1959, 142).

PHILIPPI. In 42 Brutus and Cassius joined forces at
Sardes and moved through Thrace into Macedonia, en-
camping in a good position west of Philippi, astride the
Via Egnatia and in touch with the fleet at Neapolis
(Kavalla). The legions of Antony and Octavian landed
without hindrance in Greece and marched east to face
them. Antony took the camp of Cassius, who rashly
killed himself, not knowing that Brutus had taken Octavian's; after a pause Brutus risked a second battle.
Octavian had been carried about ill, and the credit of
victory went all to Antony, who profited in a new division
of empire. Cleopatra came to him to excuse herself for not
helping with her fleet, and he started on his road to ruin
(Charlesworth in *C.A.H.* x. 22–5; for this and other battles
see also the *Schlachtenatlas*).

ACTIUM. 2 September, 31 B.C. (Dio Cassius L.; Plutarch,
Antony, 62–8; Tarn, *C.A.H.* x. 100–5; Scullard, op. cit.
176). Actium is a cape with a little town at the south side
of the Ambracian Gulf (map 16). Here Antony left his

main forces while he wintered at Patrae. Early in 31
Octavian crossed to Epirus and entrenched, despite
attempts to dislodge him, along the north side of the Gulf.
He hoped to bottle up the enemy fleet and prevent an
invasion of Italy, while he sent Agrippa to attack Antony's
supply bases in Greece. Somehow with his larger fleet
Antony lost command of the sea, and his position grew
steadily worse. His officers begged him to disengage and
retreat by land, but he chose to force the strait. Perhaps
he meant a decisive battle outside; perhaps he thought
only of escape, or this was a second plan, in case the battle
miscarried. Anyhow he had put his treasure and thousands
of picked legionaries aboard, and at an early stage Cleopatra's squadron hoisted sail for Egypt, and Antony with
forty ships followed. The fleet fought on till 300 ships left
surrendered; the army surrendered after refusing for a
week to believe that Antony had deserted it.

THE NORTHERN FRONTIER. (See also J. O. Thomson, *History of Ancient Geography*, 1948, wars with
Germans and ancient accounts of Germany, 238–47,
Danube frontier, 247–50.) In 38 B.C. Agrippa trans-
planted a German tribe (the Ubii) to the left side of the
Rhine ('to ward off others, not to be watched themselves,'
'ut arcerent, non ut custodirentur,' Tacitus, *Germania*
28). It is an early instance of a practice that became common and dangerous in the Decline, that of letting in some
barbarians to keep out worse.

Of great interest is the long effort of Augustus, mainly
employing his own stepsons Drusus and Tiberius, to
realize an Elbe–Danube rather than a Rhine–Danube
frontier. There was a climax in 9 B.C. when Drusus
penetrated through the 'Hercynian Forest' to the Elbe,
though he was accidentally killed on the way back, 'ex

magna parte domitor Germaniae.' To escape encirclement
the Marcomanni of the Main withdrew to the old 'home
of the Boii' (Bohemia), where they grew strong under an
able king, Maroboduus. In A.D. 6 Tiberius, commanding
on the Danube, launched a grand converging attack on
him, in concert with the Rhine legions, but was pulled
back by a violent revolt of the recently conquered provinces behind. The old Augustus had another shock in
A.D. 9; Varus returning with three legions from the usual
summer progress to the Weser was ambushed and destroyed in the Saltus Teutoburgiensis by the Cheruscan
chief Arminius, 'haud dubie liberator Germaniae.' (The
site is still doubtful, somewhere between Osnabrück and
Detmold.) The wailings of Augustus sound rather excessive
in the master of twenty-five legions, but the Elbe now
seemed remote. Tiberius, becoming Emperor himself in 14,
allowed some campaigns by his nephew Germanicus, who
won no adequate success and was recalled. Soon Arminius
was murdered and Maroboduus driven into exile, and it was
clear that the Germans were not dangerous meanwhile and
might safely be left to their own quarrels (Tacitus, *Annals*,
ii. 26; *Germ.* 33). But it is one of the most important
things about the Romans that they failed to conquer the
Germans. See Tacitus, *Germania*, ed. J. G. C. Anderson,
1938; *Tacitus on Britain and Germany*, translated by
Mattingly, Penguin, 1948. There was a slight advance
to an outpost line in South Germany (the German and
Raetian Limes), see R. Syme, *Cambridge Ancient History*,
xi. 158–67.

For the Danube and Trajan's addition of the large
bastion of Dacia (Transylvania) see R. P. Longden, ibid.
223–36. Trajan's Column below, photograph 125.

For the conquest of BRITAIN, Tacitus, *Agricola*, ed.

Furneaux and Anderson, 1922; *Tacitus on Britain and Germany*, translated by Mattingly, Penguin, 1948. See especially I. A. Richmond, *Roman Britain*, Penguin, 1955; Collingwood and Myres, *Roman Britain and the English Settlements*, 1937. On the statement of Tacitus 'perdomita Britannia et statim missa' see *Cambridge Ancient History*, xi. 178; on the two Walls in Britain, ibid. 522–5.

PARTHIA was not really a serious rival and some shrewd observers thought the Germans more dangerous (Tacitus, *Germ.* 37). But there was recurrent war owing to an unsatisfactory frontier and the rankling memory of Crassus. The chief trouble was Armenia, which Parthia treated as an appanage, while Rome wanted at least the 'bestowal of the kingdom'. The warlike Trajan lost patience with the usual compromise of nominal suzerainty: he annexed Armenia and even took the enemy capital Ctesiphon (Seleucia) with its golden throne. But the country rose behind him, and he died of his fatigues (A.D. 117). Hadrian at once abandoned his eastern conquests as untenable, keeping only 'Arabia,' the old Nabataean client-kingdom annexed in 106, with a 'new road' past Petra to the Red Sea. The armies of Marcus Aurelius again took Armenia and Seleucia, bringing back a terrible plague (A.D. 161–4). At the very end of the second century Septimius Severus more or less repeated Trajan's exploits, and he kept control of north Mesopotamia. The pattern of war continued even after a change of dynasty from Parthian to Sassanid or national Persian (A.D. 227). A Roman Emperor was actually taken prisoner (Valerian, 260). The prosperous caravan-city of Palmyra played a notable part in avenging this disgrace, but presumed on her service and was destroyed by Aurelian (273, see photograph, p. 124).

For the defence of 'AFRICA' see above, p. xxxvii: usually a single legion was enough. Trajan moved its headquarters a little westwards to Timgad, see photograph, p. 120.

For a Roman's notions of the JEWS see Tacitus, *Hist.* v. 2–5. For the Arch of Titus see photograph, p. 114.

For the DECLINE and the great barbarian movements beginning from the third century see Gibbon, ed. Bury, 1909; *Cambridge Medieval History*, I, 1924, etc.

A recent large-size ATLAS with many maps of great interest for ancient history is *Grosser Historischer Weltatlas*, Erster Teil, *Vorgeschichte und Altertum*, ed. H. Bengtson and others, with a volume of Commentary, *Erläuterungen* I Teil, 1953 (Bayerischer Schulbuch-Verlag). See also A. van der Heyden and H. H. Scullard, *Atlas of the Classical World*, 1959 (remarkable illustrations).

MAPS

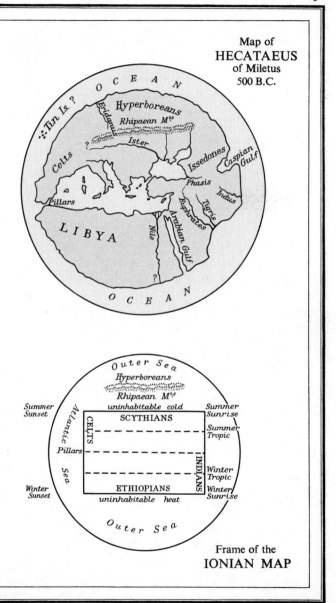

Map of
HECATAEUS
of Miletus
500 B.C.

OCEAN

Tin Is. ?

Hyperboreans

Eridanus

Rhipaean M.ᵗˢ

Celts

?

Ister

Issedones

Caspian Gulf

Phasis

Pillars

Tigris

Indus

Euphrates

LIBYA

Nile

Arabian Gulf

?

OCEAN

Outer Sea

Hyperboreans

Rhipaean M.ᵗˢ
uninhabitable cold

Summer
Sunset

Atlantic Sea

CELTS

SCYTHIANS

Summer
Sunrise

Summer
Tropic

Pillars

Winter
Tropic

INDIANS

Winter
Sunset

ETHIOPIANS
uninhabitable heat

Winter
Sunrise

Outer Sea

Frame of the
IONIAN MAP

John Bartholomew & Son, Ltd., Edinburgh

2

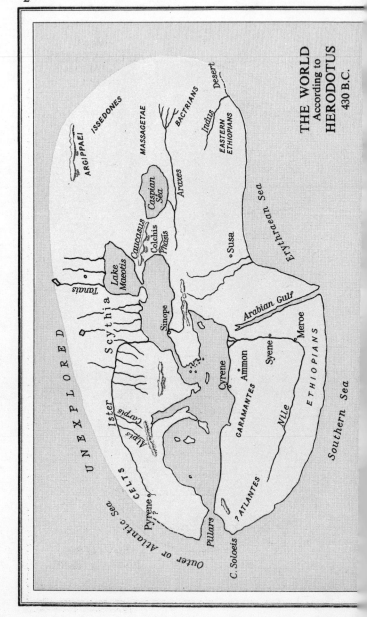

THE WORLD
According to
HERODOTUS
430 B.C.

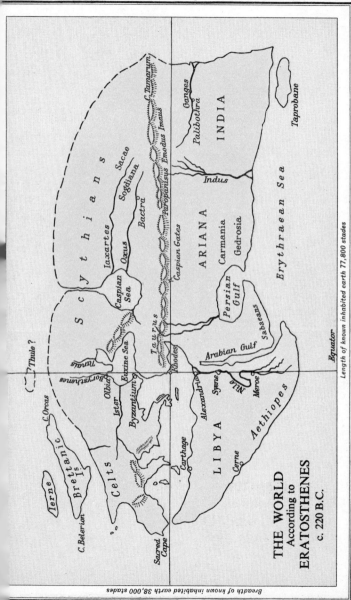

3

THE WORLD
According to
ERATOSTHENES
c. 220 B.C.

Length of known inhabited earth 77,800 stades

Breadth of known inhabited earth 38,000 stades

John Bartholomew & Son, Ltd., Edinburgh

Ierne

Brettanic Is.

C. Belerion

C. Orcas

Celts

Sacred Cape

? Thule ?

Borysthenes

Ister

Olbia

Euxine Sea

Byzantium

Tanais

Taurus

Scythians

Iaxartes

Oxus

Sacae

Sogdiana

Bactra

C. Tamarum

Paropanisus Emodus Imaus

Caspian Sea

Caspian Gates

ARIANA

Carmania

Gedrosia

Indus

Ganges

Palibothra

INDIA

Taprobane

Erythraean Sea

Persian Gulf

Sabaeans

Arabian Gulf

Rhodes

Carthage

Cerne

Alexandria

Syene

Nile

Meroe

LIBYA

Aethiopes

Equator

THE WORLD
According to
PTOLEMY
A.D. 150

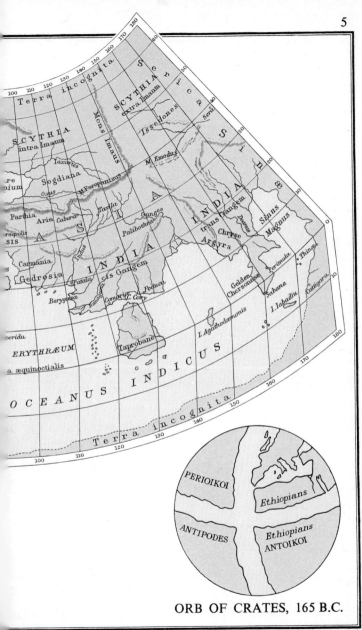

Terra incognita

SCYTHIA
intra Imaum

Taxartes

Sogdiana

Oxus

M.Paropanisus

Mons Imaus

M. Emodus

SCYTHIA
extra Imaum

Issedones

Seri

S E R I C A

Terra incognita

Parthia

Aria   Cabura

Persepolis

SIS

Taxila

A S I A

Indus

Ganges

Palibothra

INDIA
trans Gangem

Doana

Sinus
Magnus

Carmania

Gedrosia

Spatala

cis Gangem

INDIA

Argyra

Chryse

Perimula

Thinae

Barygaza

Comeria Poduca
C. Cory.

Golden
Chersonese

Sabana

Catigara

coridu

ERYTHRÆUM

a. æquinoctialis

Taprobane

I. Agathodæmonis

I. Iabadiu

O C E A N U S   I N D I C U S

Terra incognita

PERIOIKOI

Ethiopians

ANTIPODES

Ethiopians
ANTOIKOI

ORB OF CRATES, 165 B.C.

John Bartholomew & Son, Ltd., Edinburgh

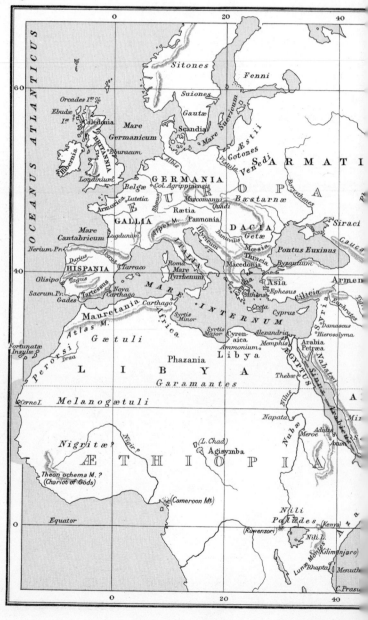

OCEANUS ATLANTICUS

Sitones

Fenni

60

Orcades I⁰ˢ

Ebudæ
I⁰ˢ Caledonia

Mare

Germanicum

Suiones

Gautæ

Scandia

Mare Suevicum

Æstii
Gotones

Venedi

ARMATI

Eburacum

Albis

Vistula

Borysthenes

BRITANNIA

Hibernia

GERMANIA

Londinium

Belgæ Col. Agrippinensis

Bastarnæ

E   U   R   O   P   A

Armorica Lutetia

Bleuus

Marcomanni

Quadi

Siraci

GALLIA

Rætia

Pannonia

DACIA

Getæ

Cauca

Cantabrica

Alpes M.

Illyricum

Danubius

Mesia

Pontus Euxinus

Mare

Lugdunum

ITALIA

Thracia

Byzantium

Nerium Pr.

Durius

Iberus

Roma

Macedonia

Asia

Armen

HISPANIA

Mare
Tyrrhenum

Athenæ

Ephesus

Cilicia

Olisipo

Tagus

Turraco

Creta

Cyprus

Sacrum Pr.

Nova
Carthago

Gades Tartessus

Euphrates

MARE · INTERNUM

Syria

Damascus

Mauretania

Carthago

Africa

Syrtis
Minor

Cyren-
aica

Hierosolyma

Atlas M.

Syrtis
Major

Alexandria

Arabia
Petræa

Fortunatæ
Insulæ

Perorsi

Gætuli

Ammonium

Memphis

Nabat

Draa

Phazania

Libya

ÆGYPTUS

Sinus Arabicus

L   I   B   Y   A

Thebæ

A

Garamantes

Cærne I.

Melanogætuli

Napata

Mir

Nubæ

Meroe Adulis

Nigritæ?

Niger

(L. Chad)

Agisymba

Axum

ÆTHIOPIA

Theonochema M.?
(Chariot of Gods)

(Cameroon Mt)

Nili
Paludes

(Kenya)

0

Equator

(Ruwenzori)

Nili L.

a

Lun Mo (Kilimanjaro)

Rhapta Menuth

C. Prasu

GREATEST EXTENT OF WORLD
KNOWN TO ANCIENTS

Silk Routes ━━━━━━
For ancient mapping see Ptolemy (Pages 4-5)

60   80   100

Norossus M. (Ural)

Daix

S C Y T H I A

Alani *r s i* cis Imaum

Jaxartes

Oxianus L.

Chorasmii

Oxus Scythicus M.   *Silk Routes*

HUNS
(HIUNG-NU)

S C Y T H I A

Mare Caspium

Dahæ   *Oxus*   *Maracanda*   *Kashgar*   trans Imaum

Parthia   Bactriana   Aspacaræ

R. *Yellow* *To Sea*

40

A R I A N A   *Indoscythia*   A S I A   *Imaus M.*   I   A   Bautæ

SERICA

Persepolis   Drangiana   *India*

Emodus M.

Persis   Gedrosia

SINÆ

Sin Persicus   *Pattala*   *Palibothra*   *Ganges*

Argyre

B I A   ix   *Maca*   I N D I A   cis Gangem   *trans Gangem* A I A

Omanitæ   *Ozene*   *Barygaza*

Sinus Magnus

20

Monsoon Mare   *Simylla*   *Ariaca*   *Masolia*

Sailing

C. Syagros   Erythræum

Poduca

Sinus Perimulicus

I. Dioscoridu

Aromata Pr.

Muziris   *Modura*

Comaria Pr.   Taprobane I.

Chryse
Cherson:

O C E A N U S   I N D I C U S

Sabana

0

Jabadiu I.

Longitude East 60 of Greenwich   80   100

© – John Bartholomew & Son, Ltd., Edinburgh

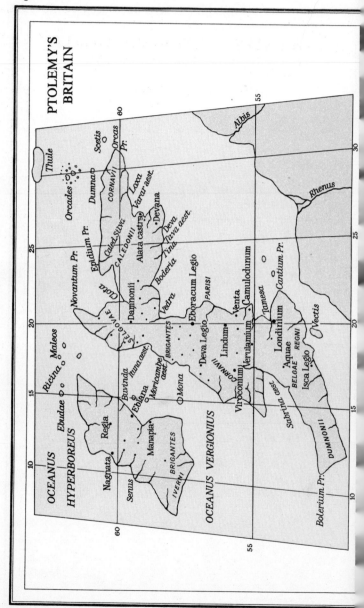

PTOLEMY'S BRITAIN

SCENE OF
OLDEST EMPIRES

English Miles

0   100   200   300   400   500

Longitude East 35 of Greenwich

© – John Bartholomew & Son, Ltd., Edinburgh

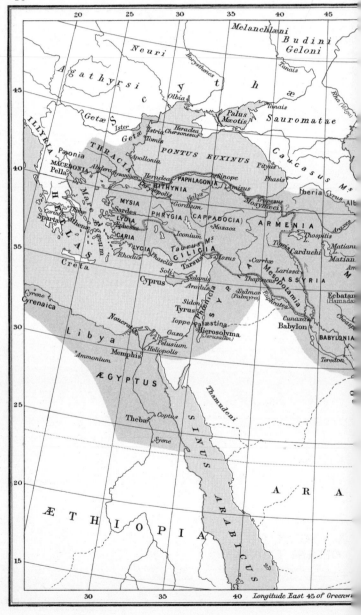

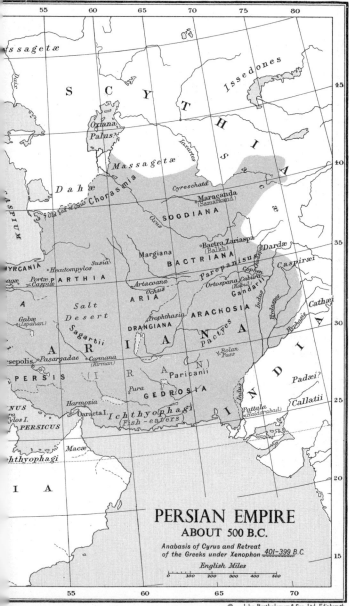

PERSIAN EMPIRE
ABOUT 500 B.C.

Anabasis of Cyrus and Retreat
of the Greeks under Xenophon 401–399 B.C.

English Miles

0   100   200   300   400   500

© – John Bartholomew & Son, Ltd., Edinburgh

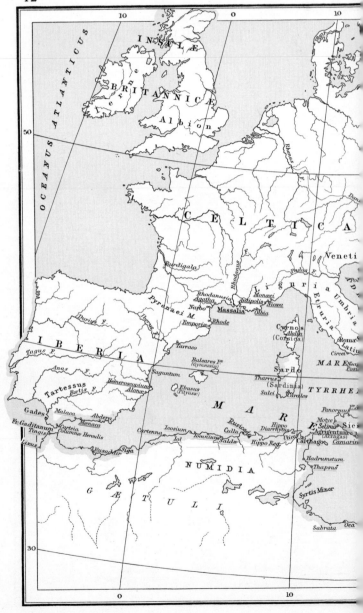

INSVLÆ
BRITANNICÆ
Albion
Erin

OCEANUS ATLANTICUS

50

CELTICA

Veneti

Burdigala

Liguria
Etruria
Umbria

Pyrenaei M.
Rhodanusia
Agatha
Narbo Massalia
Emporiæ Rhode
Monaci
Antipolis Nicæa
Olbia

Durius F.

IBERIA

Tagus F.

Tarraco

Cyrnos
(Corsica)
Alalia

Roma
Latiu

Circeii

Anas F.

Saguntum
Baleares Iæ
(Gymnesiæ)

MARE

Nea
Posi

Tartessus Betis F.
Hemerosyavium
Alonæ
Ebusus
(Tityusæ)

Tharrus
(Sardinia) Sarilo
Sulci Carales

TYRRHE

Gades
Malaca Abdera
Fr:Gaditanum Marteia Mænaca
Tingis Columnæ Herculis

MARE

Panormus
Motye
Selinus
Agrigentum
(Acragas)

Sici
Camarin

Cartenna Icosium
Iol Iomnium Salda

Rusicca
Cullu
Hippo
Diarrhytus
Utica
Hippo Reg. Carthago

Lixus
Rusaddir Siga

NUMIDIA

Hadrumetum
Thapsus

GÆTULI

Syrtis Minor

Sabrata Oea

30

0   10

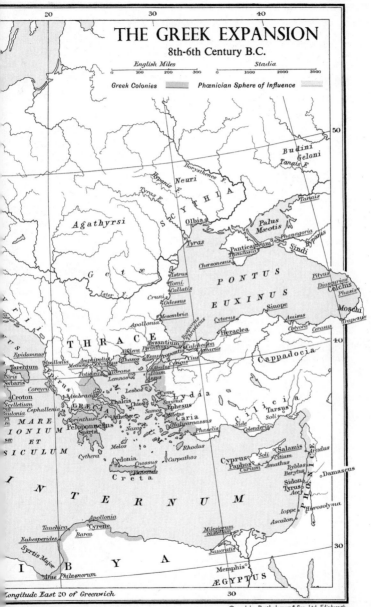

THE GREEK EXPANSION
8th-6th Century B.C.

English Miles
0 100 200 300

Stadia
0 1000 2000 3000

Greek Colonies   Phœnician Sphere of Influence

Budini
Geloni
Tanais F.
SCYTHIA
Neuri
Borysthenes F.
Hypanis F.
Tyras F.
Agathyrsi
Olbia
Palus Mæotis
Phanagoria
Hypanis
Panticapaeum
Sindi
Theudosia
Tyras
Getæ
Chersonesus
Pityus
Dioscurias
Colchis
Phasis
Moschi
Ister F.
PONTUS
Istrus
Tomi
Callatis
Cruni
Odessus
EUXINUS
Drapezus
Mesembria
Sinope
Cytorus
Amisus
Cotyora
Cerasus
Apollonia
Bosporus
Thynicus
Heraclea
THRACE
Byzantium
Calchedon
Perinthus
Astacus
Selera
Amphipolis
Thasos
Propontis
Cius
Methone
Olynthus
Abydus
Cappadocia
Tarentum
Apollonia
Potidaea
Torone
Ilium
Siris
Lemnos
Assus
Sybaris
Epidamnus
Epirus
Cyme
Croton
Coreyra
Lesbos
Lydia
Ambracia
Thalcis
Chios
Smyrna
Scylletium
Cephallenia
GREECE
Ephesus
Caulonia
Corinthus
Athenæ
Samos
Miletus
Cilicia
Tarsus
MARE
Peloponnesus
Caria
Soli
IONIUM
Sparta
Naxos
Halicarnassus
ET
Melos
Phaselis
Side
SICULUM
Celenderis
Cythera
Rhodus
INTERNUM
Cydonia
Cnossus
Carpathos
Cyprus
Soli
Salamis
Paphos
Citium
Phæstus
Curium
Amathus
Creta
Byblos
Damascus
Berytus
Sidon
Tyrus
Ace
Tauchera
Apollonia
Cyrene
Ioppe
Hierosolyma
Euhesperides
Barca
Ascalon
Syrtis Major
Milesiorum castellum
L I B Y A
Naucratis
Arae Philaenorum
Memphis
ÆGYPTUS

Longitude East 20 of Greenwich

© – John Bartholomew & Son. Ltd.. Edinburgh

GRAECIA

English Miles

0 10 20 30 40 50

Greek Stadia

0 100 200 300 400 500

I A Amphipolis
Strigibus *Argilus* *Eion* *Galepsus* Thasos
pollonia *Apollonia* Thasos *Maronea* *Mesombria* *Dorisus* *Zeshrus* *Enos*
pageirus Strymon Strymonicus S. *Sarpedon Pr.* *Melas* S Cardia *Imgilmache*
ice *Camp of Xerxes* Samothrace *Alopeconnesus* *Callipoli* Pariym
Acanthus Singiticus S. Samothrace *Limnae* *Sestos* Lampsacus *Percote*
Sithonia Athos M. Imbros *Abydus* *Gergithus*
S Derrhis Pr. Nymphium Pr. Imbros **Mare** Hellespontus *Rhoeteum* 40
Pr. Icos Myrina Lemnos *Sigeum* *Ilium, Troja*
Peparethos Halonnesus Tenedos *Scamander*
rinthus *Alexandria Troas* *Antandros* Adramyttium
  Scyros Scyros *Chryse* *Gargara* *Assos*
  Nea *Lectum Pr.* *Adramyttenus*
U B Cyme Psyra *Methymna* Pitane Elæa
Chalcis *Eretria* *Antissa* Lesbos *Mytilene* *Elæates* 39
Oropus Chios *Eresus* *Pyrrha* *Cyme*
Parnes M. *Cardamyle* Phocaea
Asopus *Decelea* Marathon *Caphereus Pr.* Chios *Hermaeus S.*
Pentelicus M. Carystus *Erythrae* Clazomena Smyrna
Athenæ *Hymettus M.* *Gerastus Pr.* Andros Teos Lebedos 38
Halonius Helene vel Macris *Gabrion* *Coryceum Pr.*
Sunium Pr. *Prasiæ* Andros *Cantharium Pr.* Samos
Calauria Gyaros Tenos Icaria *Samos*
Ceos *Tenos* *Oenoe*
Calauria Sin. Cythnos Syros Myconos Patmos Lepsia 37
Hydrea *Cythnos* Rhenea *Myconos* Leros
Mare Delos **Icarium Mare**
Seriphos Paros Naxos *Donussa* *Lebinthos*
Minoa Oliaros *Paros* Naxos Calymna
Siphnos *Minoa* Cos
Cimolos *Prepesinthos* Heraclea Amorgos
Ephyra *Polyægos* *Sicinos* *Ios* Astypalæa
Melos Ios Anaphe
Pholegandros Thera *Therasia* *Thera*

Doric	Ionic
Æolian & Achæan	

© – John Bartholomew & Son, Ltd, Edinburgh

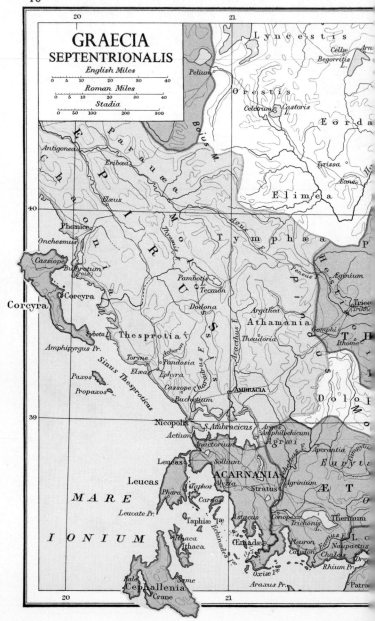

© – John Bartholomew & Son, Ltd., Edinburgh

2

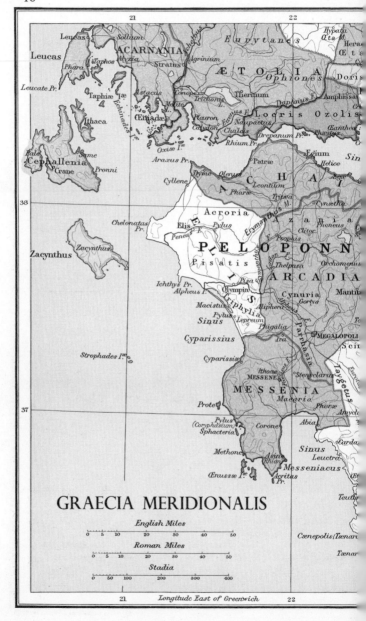

21   22

Leucas · Sollium · Anactorium

ACARNANIA

Leucas · Phara · Taphos · Alyzia · Agrinium · Stratus

Eurytanes · Hypata · Œta

ÆTOLIA · Heraea · Œta

Leucate Pr. · Taphiæ Iæ · Astacus · Conope · Trichonis L. · Thermum · *Ophiones* · Doris

Echinades I. · Matio · Daphnus Pr. · Amphissa

Ithaca · Œniadæ · Pleuron · Calydon · Chalcis · **Locris Ozolis**

Oxiae I. · Rhium Pr. · Drepanum Pr. · Œanthea · Phaestus

Pale · Same · Araxus Pr. · Patræ · Ægium · Sin

Cephallenia · Crane · Pronni · Ægira · Helice

Echinades I.

Dyme · Olerus · **ACHAI**

Cyllene · Leontium · Phara

Zacynthus · Chelonatas Pr. · Acroria · Tritæa M. · Cynætha

Elis · Pylus · *Azania* · Pheneus

Zacynthus · Elis · Peneus · Erymanthus · Cleitor · Psophis

P E L O P O N N

Pisatis · Thelpusa · Orchomenus

Ichthys Pr. · Pisa · **ARCADIA**

Alpheus I. · Olympia · Cynuria · Mantin

Macistus · Alpheus · Gortys

Pylus · **Triphylia**

Sinus · Lepreum · Phigalia · Parrhasia

Cyparissius · Ira · **MEGALOPOLI**

Strophades Iæ · Cyparissiæ · Ithome · Stenyclarus · Sci

MESSENE

MESSENIA · Taÿgetus

Protë · Macaria · Pheræ · Amycl

Pylus · Abia · Carda

(Coryphasium) · Corone · **Sinus**

Sphacteria · Leuctra

Methone · Asine · **Messeniacus** · Œt

Rhium · Teuth

Œnussæ I. · Acritas Pr.

GRAECIA MERIDIONALIS

English Miles

0   5   10   20   30   40   50

Roman Miles

0   5   10   20   30   40   50

Stadia

0   50   100   200   300   400

Cænepolis/Tænar

Tænar

21   *Longitude East of Greenwich*   22

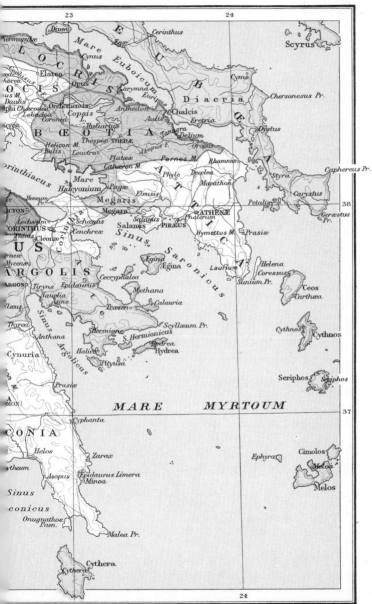

Map content (labels):

Scyrus, Cerinthus, Ægæ, Dium, Cynus, Mare Euboicum, Chersonesus Pr., Thermopylæ, Elatea, Opus, Carymna, Anthedon, Cymē, LOCRIS, Daulis M., Chæronea, Orchomenus, Copais L., Chalcis, Diacria, Eretria, Aulis, Tanagra, Delium, Dystus, BŒOTIA, Thespiæ, THEBÆ, Coronea, Haliartus, Leuctra, Helicon M., Plataeæ, Parnes M., Oropus, Rhamnus, Caphereus Pr., Cithæron M., Phyle, Decelea, Styra, Mare Halcyonium, Pagæ, Eleusis, Marathon, Carystus, Megaris, ATTICA, Petaliæ I., Geræstus Pr., Megara, Salamis, ATHENÆ, Schœnus, Cenchreæ, Salamis, PIRÆUS, Phalerum, Prasiæ, Lechæum, CORINTHUS, Sinus Saronicus, Hymettus M., Cleonæ, Helena, Ægina, Ægina, Laurium, Coressus, Cecryphalea, Sunium Pr., Ceos, Carthæa, Mycenæ, ARGOLIS, Tiryns, Epidaurus, Methana, Nauplia, Asine, Calauria, Trœzen, Cythnos, Cythnos, Thyrea, Hermione, Scyllæum Pr., Anthana, Halice, S. Hermionicus, Pityusa, Hydrea, Hydrea, Cynuria, Argolicus Sinus, Seriphos, Seriphos, Prasiæ, MARE MYRTOUM, Cyphanta, LACONIA, Helos, Zarax, Ephyra, Cimolos, Melos, Gytheum, Asopus, Epidaurus Limera, Minoa, Melos, Sinus Laconicus, Onugnathos Paen., Malea Pr., Cythera, Cythera

© – John Bartholomew & Son, Ltd. Edinburgh

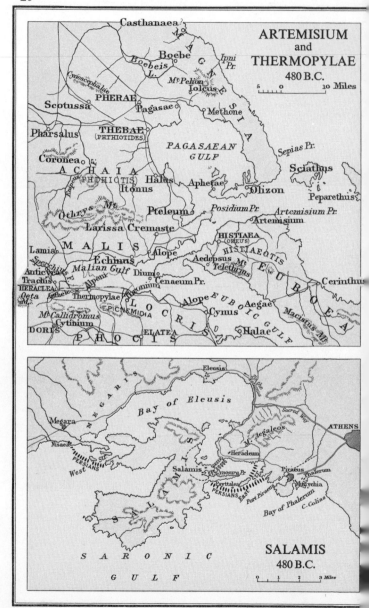

ARTEMISIUM
and
THERMOPYLAE
480 B.C.

5   0   10 Miles

Casthanaea?
Boebe
Boebeis L.
Cynoscephalae
M. Pelion
Ipni Pr.
Iolcus
M A G N E S I A
PHERAE
Scotussa
Pagasae
Methone
Pharsalus
THEBAE
(PHTHIOTIDES)
PAGASAEAN
GULF
Sepias Pr.
Coronea
A C H A I A
(PHTHIOTIS)
Halus
Aphetae
Sciathus
Itonus
Olizon
Peparethus
M. Othrys
Pteleum
Posidium Pr.
Artemisium Pr.
Larissa Cremaste
Artemisium
HISTIAEA
(OREUS)
Lamia
M A L I S
Alope
HISTIAEOTIS
Spercheus
Echinus
Aedepsus
M. Telethrius
E U B O E A
Anticyra
Malian Gulf
Diume
Trachis
Alpeni
Cenaeum Pr.
Cerinthus
HERACLEA
Oeta
Anthele
Thermopylae
Dromium
Alope
E U B O I C
Aegae
Macistus Mt.
M. Callidromus
EPICNEMIDIA
L O C R I S
Cynus
G U L F
Cytinium
Halae
DORIS
P H O C I S
ELATEA

SALAMIS
480 B.C.

0   1   2   3 Miles

Eleusis
M E G A R I S
Bay of Eleusis
Cephisus
Sacred Way
Megara
ATHENS
Nisaea
M. Aegaleos
West
PERSIANS
Heracleum
Salamis
Cynosura Pr.
Piraeus
Phalerum
S A L A M I S
Psyttalea
PERSIANS
Port Piraeus
Munychia
Bay of Phalerum
C. Colias
S A R O N I C
G U L F

John Bartholomew & Son, Ltd., Edinb

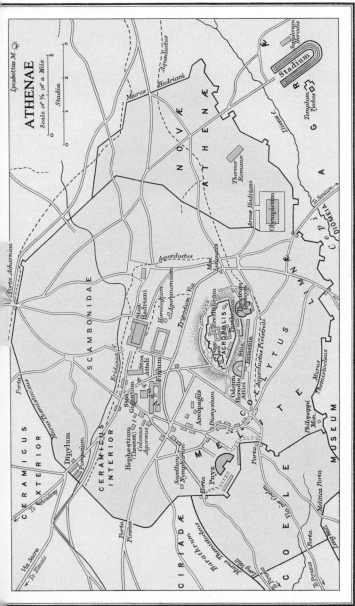

ATHENAE

Scale of ¼ of a Mile

Stadia

© – John Bartholomew & Son, Ltd. Edinburgh

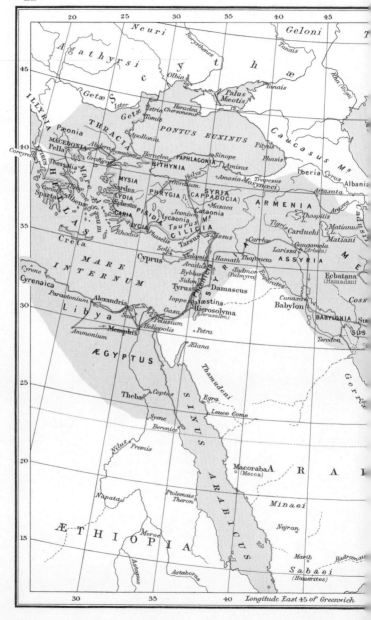

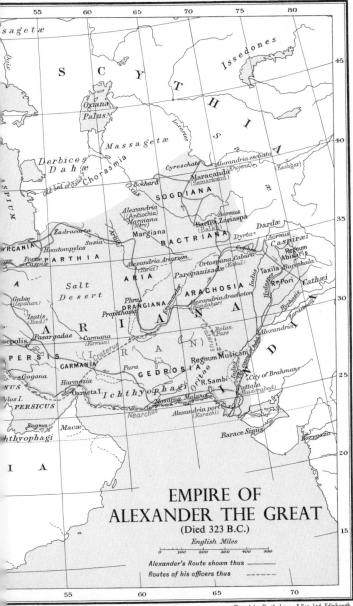

23

EMPIRE OF
ALEXANDER THE GREAT
(Died 323 B.C.)

English Miles

0   100   200   300   400   500

Alexander's Route shown thus ——————
Routes of his officers thus — — — — —

© — John Bartholomew & Son, Ltd., Edinburgh

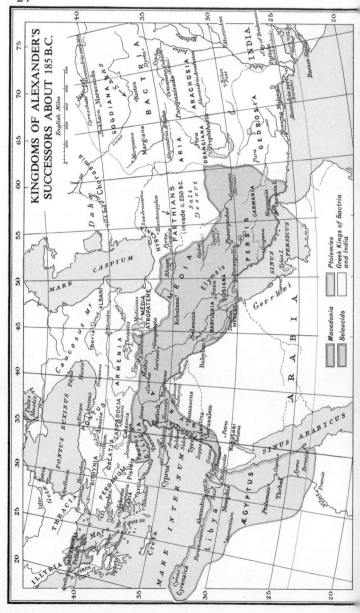

KINGDOMS OF ALEXANDER'S
SUCCESSORS ABOUT 185 B.C.

English Miles

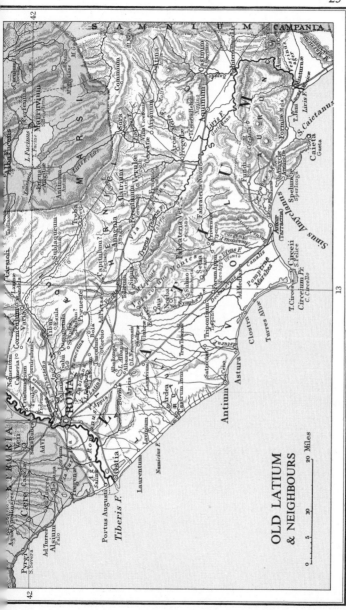

OLD LATIUM
& NEIGHBOURS

20 Miles

0   5   10   20

John Bartholomew & Son, Ltd. Edinburgh

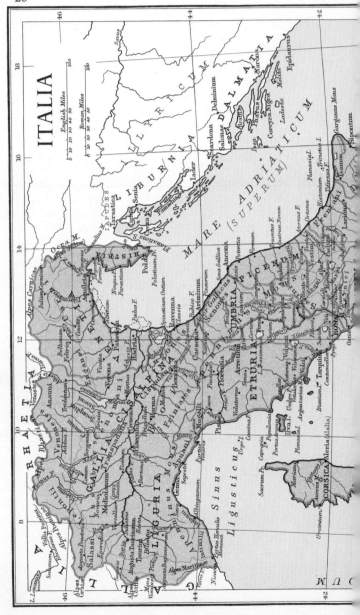

ITALIA

English Miles
0 10 20 30 40 50   100

Roman Miles
0 10 20 30 40 50   100

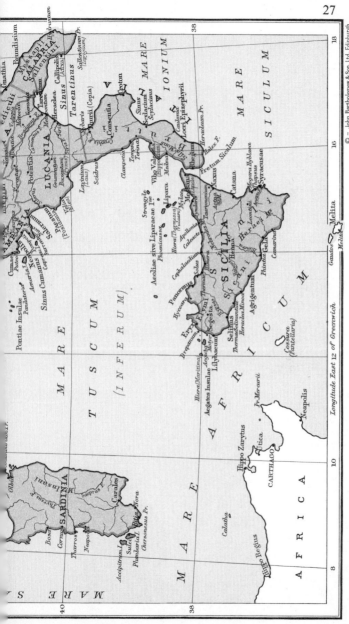

Brundisium
Amathia
Messapii Λ Γ· άζου Iapygium Pr.
CALABRIA
SALLENTINI
Hydruntum
Callipolis
Uxentum (Leuca?)
Sallentinum Pr.
(Iapygium)

LUCANIA
Heraclea
Metapontum
Potentia
Siris
Thurii (Copia)
Sinus
Tarentinus
Croton

Buxentum
Sybaris
Crathis f.
Consentia
MARE
IONIUM

Grumentum
Laginium (Clous)
Scidrus
Clampetia
Tempsa
Terina

BRUTTII

Vibo Valentia
Hipponium
Medma

Sinus
Scylacius
Scylacium
Caulonia
Locri Epizephyrii

Rhegium
Fretum Siculum
Heracleum Pr.

TUSCUM

(INFERUM)

Aeoliae sive Liparaeae ins.
Strongyle
Lipara
Hierα (Vulcania)
Phoenicussa

Mylae
Messana
Tauromenium
Naxus
Aetna M.
Catana

MARE
SICULUM

Cephaloedium
Calacte
Apollonia
Tyndaris

Panormus
Solus

Herbessus
Hybla
Megaris
Leontini

Syracusae

Hyccara
Egesta (Segesta)
Eryx
Drepanum
Entella
Halicyae
Selinus
Lilybaeum
Motya

SICANI

Gela
Phintia Gela
Camarina

AFRICUM

Agrigentum
Thermae Selinuntinae
Heraclea Minoa

Pontiae Insulae
Pandateria

Cumae
Puteoli
Misenum Pr.
Baiae Neapolis
Nola
Sinus Cumanus
Surrentum
Capreae
Posidonia
(Paestum)
Salernum

CAMPANIA

Hiera(Maritima)
Aegates Insulae
Aegusa
Cossura
(Pantellaria)

MARE

A F R I C U M

Gaudos

Melita

Melita

Longitude East 12 of Greenwich

SARDINIA

Olbia
Corvus
Bosa
Thyrsus f.
Caralis
Sacrus f.

Accipitrum P.
Plumbaria I.
Tharros
Neapo
Sulci
Bitia
Nora
Chersonesus Pr.

MARE

Hippo Zarytus
Utica
CARTHAGO

Fr. Mercurii
Neapolis
Calatha

A F R I C A

Hippo Regius

© – John Bartholomew & Son, Ltd. Edinburgh

MARE

38
40
38
8
10
16
18

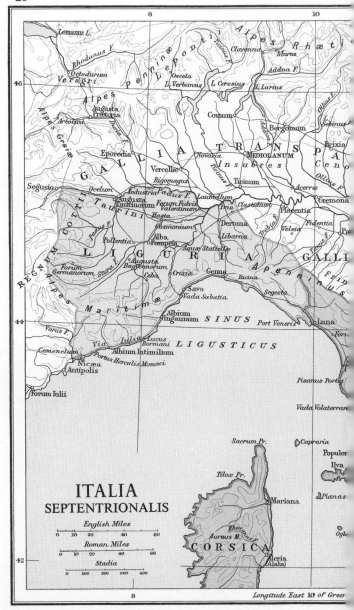

Lemanus L.

Rhodanus F.

Octodurum

Veragri

Alpes Penninæ

Lepontii

Alpes Rhæti

Ticinus

Clavenna

Muras

Addua F.

Oscela

L. Verbanus

L. Ceresius

L. Larius

46

Augusta
Prætoria

Alpes

Ariolica

Duria F.

Comum

Addua F.

Bergomum

Ollius F.

L.
Sebinus

Brixia

Alpes Graia

GALLIA

Eporedia

Vercellæ

Novaria

MEDIOLANUM

TRANSPA
Ceno

Insubres

Ollius F.

Segusio

Ocelum

Industria

Taurini

Padus F.

Rigomagus

Ticinus

Ticinum

Laumellum

Acerræ

Cremona

Augusta
Taurinorum

Forum Fulvii
Valentinum

Tria

Clastidium

Placentia

REGNUM COTTII

Hasta

Casmonium

Dertona

Libarna

Veleia

Fidentia

Padus F.

Alba
Pompeia

Pollentia

Aquæ Statiellæ

LIGUR

IA

Tanus F.

GALLI

Pa

Forum
Germanorum

Augusta
Bagiennorum

Stura F.

Ceba

Crixia

Genua

Ricina

Apenninus

Frin

Savo

Vada Sabatia

Segesta

Alpes

Maritimæ

Albium
Ingaunum

SINUS

Port Veneris

Luna

44

Varus F.

Via
Iulia

Lucus
Bormani

LIGUSTICUS

For

Cemenelum

Albium Intimilium

Nicæa

Portus Herculis Monœci

Antipolis

Pisanus Portus

Forum Iulii

Vada Volaterran

Sacrum Pr.

Capraria

Populon

Ilva

Tilox Pr.

Planas

ITALIA
SEPTENTRIONALIS

Mariana

English Miles

0 10 20   40   60

Roman Miles

0   10   20   40   60

Stadia

0   100   200   300   400

Rhotani F.

Aureus M.

CORSICA

Ogl

Aleria
(Alalia)

42

8

10

© – John Bartholomew & Son. Ltd. Edinburgh

MARE ADRIATICUM

MARE

42

18

16

14

40

Aternum

Ortona

Buca

Urium

Garganus M.

Sipontum

Salapia

Aufidus F.

Canusium

Barium

Gnathia

Butuntum Caelia

Poediculi
(Peucetii)

L. Rube

Brundisium

Tarentum Uria

Aletium

CALABRIA

Lupiae

Neretum

Uxentum

Hydruntum
Castrum
Veretum

Iapygium s.
Salentinum Pr.

Sallentini

S. Callipolis
Manduria

SINUS

TARENTINUS

Ansxa

Metapontum

Siris

Heraclea

Pandosia

Acia

Siris F.

Neaethus

Thurii

Murenum

(Trans Murenum)

LUCANIA

Sybaris

Sabrus

Acalandrus

Venusia

Bantia

Potentia

Forum
Popilii

Atina

Volcei

Velia (Elea)

Buxentum

Posidium Pr.

Palinuri Pr.

Paestanus
Sinus

Paestum

Surrentum

Sinus

Cumanus

Sinus

Misenum

Puteoli

KAPOLIS

Cumae

Nola

Vesuvius M.

Compsa

Aquilonia

CAMPANIA

Suessula

Capua

Volturnus F.

Teanum

Cales

Telesia

Casilinum

Beneventum

Caudium

Saticula

Abellinum

Hirpini

SAMNIUM

Bovianum

Venafrum

Aesernia

Larinum

Frentani

Teanum Apulum

Luceria

Arpi

APULIA

Ausculum

Aecae

Herdonia

Vibinum

Daunii

Sidicini

Aufidena

Corfinium

Sulmo

Paeligni

Marsi

Marruvium

Anxanum

Teate

Marrucini

Vestini

Interamna

Amiternum

Reate

Nursia

Sabini

Interocrea

Aveia

Alba Fucens

Lacus Fucinus

Carseoli

Aequi

Trebula

Tibur

Praeneste

M. Albanus

Bovillae

ROMA

Ostia

Portus
Augusti

Fidenae

Veii

Falerii

Nar F.

Tiberis F.

Crustumerium

Antemnae

Laurentum

Lavinium

Ardea

Antium

Astura

Circei

Pontiae Insulae

Tarracina

Formiae

Fundi

Caieta

Minturnae

Sinuessa

Vescia

Fabrateria

Aquinum

Casinum

Interamna

Arpinum

Sora

Fregellae

Frusino

Anagnia

Ferentinum

Signia

Cora

Velitrae

Suessa

Nova

Setia

Appia Via

LATIUM

Pandateria

Aenaria

Pithecusa

Caprea

MARE

Pontia Insula

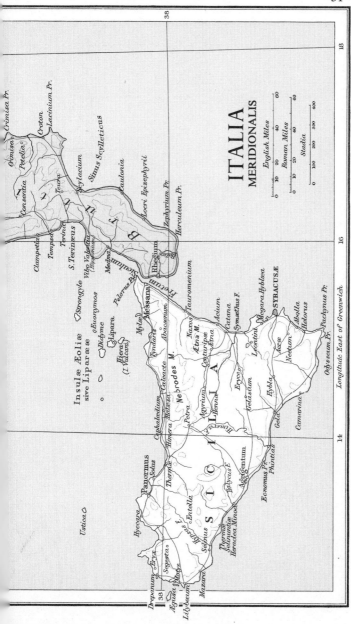

38

18

ITALIA
MERIDIONALIS

English Miles
0   10   20   30   40   50   60

Roman Miles
0   10   20   30   40   50   60

Stadia
0   100   200   300   400

16

Longitude East of Greenwich

14

© – John Bartholomew & Son, Ltd., Edinburgh

Orinisa Crimisa Pr.
Croton
Petelia Lacinium Pr.
Consentia
B R U T I I
Tempsa
Terina Scylacium
Clampetia Sinus Scylleticus
S. Terinaeus
Caulonia
Who Valenta
Hipponium Locri Epizephyrii
Medma
Scyllaeum Zephyrium Pr.
Rhegium Herculeum Pr.
Strongyle Fretum
Euonymos Pelorus Pr.
Didyme
Lipara Mylae
Hiera Messana
(I. Vulcani) Tyndaris Abacaenum
Insulae Aeoliae Nebrodes M. Naxos Tauromenium
sive Liparae Cephaloedium Aleaeae Aetna M. Acium
Petra Centuripe Aetna Catana
Himera F. Agyrium Leontini Symaethus F.
Ustica Thermae Herbita Megara Hyblaea
Solus Eryces STRACUSAE
Panormus Enna Galaxium Abolla
Hyccara Acrae Helorus
S I C I L I A Neetum Pachynus Pr.
Thermae Talycus F. Hybla
Entella Gela Odysseum Pr.
Segesta Selinus F. Agrigentum
Drepanum Hypsas F. Camarina
353 Eryx Selinus Phintias
Acytus Halycus Gela Economus Pr.
Lilybaeum Thermae
Mazara Selinuntia
Heraclea Minoa

ROMAN EMPIRE
AT THE DEATH OF CÆSAR

English Miles
Roman Miles

Roman Territory and Provinces
Protected States

25 30 35 40 45 50 55 60

SARMATIA

55

50

45

AORSI

ALANI

Caspium

Borysthenes Fl.

Hypanis

Maeotis
Palus

Tanais Fl.

Rha Fl.

Olbia

Tyras

Hypanis

Sinda

Tauri

Achillis I.

Heraclea
Chersonesus

Caucasus Mons

Albania

Cyrus Fl.

Istropolis

PONTUS EUXINUS

Pityus

Dioscurias

Colchis

Iberia

Phasis

Araxes Fl.

40

Tomis

Odessus

Sinope

Heraclea Pontica

Trapezus

Artaxata

ARMENIA

Apollonia

Amasia

Pontus

Nicopolis

Satala

Ararat M.

Atropatene

MEDIA

THRACIA

Philippopolis

Byzantium

BITHYNIA

Iris Fl.

Halys Fl.

Tarsum Fl.

Amida

Gordyene

35

Perinthus

Nicaea

Ancyra

Pessinus

CAPPADOCIA

Nisibis

Singara

Nineveh

Mysia

Lydia

Phrygia

Lycaonia

Caesarea Mazaca

Comana

Elegeia

Edessa

Carrhae

Hatra

REGNUM

Sardes

CILICIA

Iconium

Tyana

MESOPOTAMIA

PARTHORUM

Ephesus

Caria

PAMPHYLIA

Tarsus

Seleucia

Apollonia

LYCIA

Attalia

Issus

Antiochia

Zeugma

Dura

Ctesiphon

Rhodos

Myra

Salamis

Laodicea

Apamea

Circesium

Seleucia

BABYLONIA

Babylon

Creta

CYPRUS

Paphos

Arados

Tripolis

SYRIA

Emesa

Palmyra

Damascus

Euphrates Fl.

Charax

MARE

Sidon

Tyrus

Heliopolis

Ptolemais

Caesarea

Neapolis

Bostra

Alexandria

Pelusium

Hierosolyma

Petra

ARABIA

PETRAEA

Elana

25

Marmarica

Paraetonium

Memphis

Heliopolis

Arsinoë

Aelana

Sinus M.

ARABIA

Ammon

Heracleopolis

Antinoe

Arabicus Sinus

Hermopolis

AEGYPTUS

Abydos

Tentyra

Thebae

Lotopolis

Tropic of Cancer

Berenice

Philae I.

Syene

A

ude East 25 of Greenwich 30 35 40

© – John Bartholomew & Son, Ltd, Edinburgh

3

34

ROMAN EMPIRE
AT ITS GREATEST EXTENT
SECOND CENTURY A.D.

English Miles

Roman Miles

© – John Bartholomew & Son, Ltd., Edinburgh

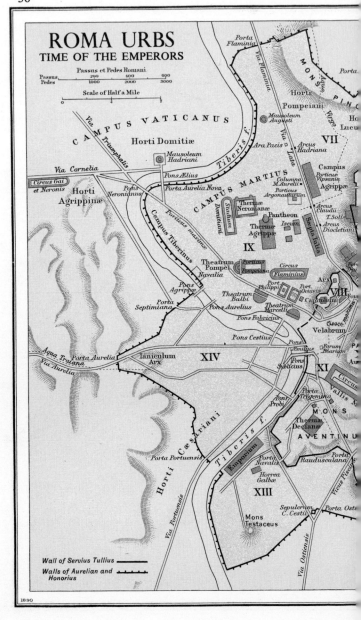

ROMA URBS
TIME OF THE EMPERORS

Passus et Pedes Romani

Passus 200 400 600
Pedes 1000 2000 3000

Scale of Half a Mile

CAMPUS VATICANUS

Horti Domitiæ

Via Cornelia

Via Triumphalis

Mausoleum Hadriani

Pons Ælius

Porta Aurelia Nova

Circus Gai et Neronis

Horti Agrippinæ

Pons Neronianus

Pons Agrippæ

Porta Septimiana

Porticus maxima

Campus Tiberinus

Theatrum Pompei
Navalia

Theatrum Balbi

Pons Aurelius

Pons Cestius

Aqua Traiana
Porta Aurelia
Via Aurelia

Ianiculum
Arx

XIV

Horti Cæsariani

Porta Portuensis

Via Portuensis

Tiberis f.

Porta Flaminia

Via Flaminia

MONS PINC

Porta

Hortii Pompeiani

Aqua Virgo

Ho
Lucu

Mausoleum Augusti

Ara Pacis

Arcus Hadriana

Via Lata

VII

Campus

CAMPUS MARTIUS

Columna M. Aurelii

Porticus Vipsaniæ
Porticus Argonautarum

Porticus Agrippæ

Thermæ Neronianæ

Stadium Domitiani

Pantheon
Iseum

Arcus Claudii
T. Solis
Arcus Diocletiani

Thermæ Agrippæ

Septa Iulia

IX

Porticus Pompeiana

Circus Flaminius

Arx

Port. Philippi

Port. Octaviæ

VIII

Theatrum Marcelli

Capitolium

Pons Fabricius

Pons Æmilius

Pons

Velabrum

Forum Boarium

XI

Pons Sublicius

Vallis M

Circus M

Pons Probi

Porta Trigemina

MONS

Thermæ Decianæ

AVENTINU

Emporium

Porta Navalis

Porta Raudusculana

Horrea Galbæ

XIII

Sepulcrum C. Cestii

Porta Ost

Porta Ostiensis

Mons Testaceus

Via Ostiensis

Vicus

Wall of Servius Tullius ———

Walls of Aurelian and Honorius ·—·—·—·

1890

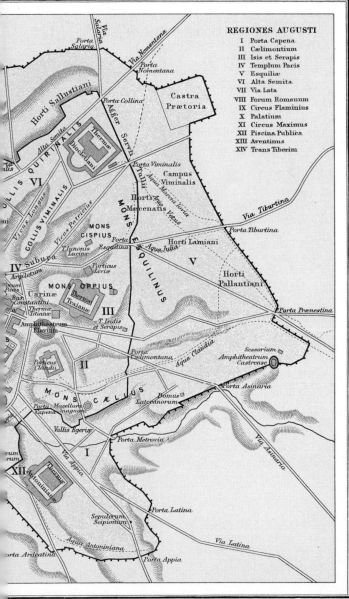

REGIONES AUGUSTI

I	Porta Capena
II	Cælimontium
III	Isis et Serapis
IV	Templum Pacis
V	Esquiliæ
VI	Alta Semita
VII	Via Lata
VIII	Forum Romanum
IX	Circus Flaminius
X	Palatium
XI	Circus Maximus
XII	Piscina Publica
XIII	Aventinus
XIV	Trans Tiberim

Via Salaria

Porta Salaria

Via Nomentana

Porta Nomentana

Horti Sallustiani

Castra Prætoria

Porta Collina

Alta Semita

Agger Servii

Thermæ Diocletiani

QUIRINALIS

VI

Porta Viminalis

Campus Viminalis

Aqua Marcia Iovia

Via Tiburtina

Horti Mæcenatis

Aqua Anio Vetus

Porta Tiburtina

Vicus Longus

COLLIS VIMINALIS

Vicus Patricius

MONS CISPIUS

MONS

Porta Esquilina

Horti Lamiani

IV Subura

T[l]unonis Lucinæ

Aqua Julia

V

EQUILINUS

Porticus Liviæ

Argiletum

Horti Pallantiani

[D]cum Pins

Carinæ

MONS OPPIUS

Thermæ Traianæ

III

Porta Prænestina

[Basi] Constantini

Thermæ Titianæ

T. Isidis et Serapis

Amphitheatrum Flavium

Sessorium

Amphitheatrum Castrense

Porticus Claudii

II

Aqua Claudia

Porta Cælimontana

MONS CÆLIUS

Porta Asinaria

Domus Lateranorum

Porta Macellum Capena magnum

Vallis Egeriæ

Via Asinaria

Porta Metrovia

I

Via Appia

XII

Thermæ [A]ntoninianæ

Via Latina

Sepulcrum Scipionum

Porta Latina

Aqua Antoniniana

[P]orta Ardeatina

Porta Appia

© – John Bartholomew & Son. Ltd. Edinburgh

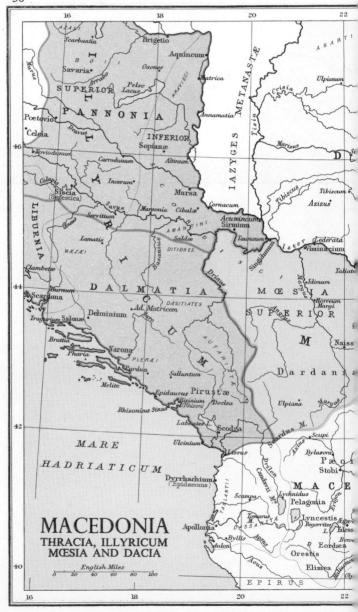

16   18   20   22

Scarbantia   **Brigetio**
ARAVI   BOII   **Aquincum**
Savaria   *Osones*   *Matrica*
Arrabo   Pelso   ANARTI
Marus   SUPERIOR   Lacus   Ulpianum
P A N N O N I A   ARAVISCI   METANASTÆ
Poetovio   *Annamatia*   Crisia
Celeia   Dravus   **INFERIOR**   Tisia   D
46   Noviodunum   Sopianæ   IAZYGES   Marisus
Carrodunum   *Altinum*   Tibiscus   Tibiscum
Colapis   Incerum   C   Azizus
Siscia   **Mursa**
(Segestica)   Savus   Cornacum
LIBURNIA   Servitium   Marsonia   Cibalæ   Acumincum
Enus   AMANTINI   Sirmium
Lamatis   Taurunum   Ister   Lederata
MÆZÆI   Saldæ   D   Singidunum   Viminacium
Bassanius   DITIONES   S   C   Idimum
Clambetæ   Margus
44   Burnum   **D A L M A T I A**   DÆSITIATES   **MŒSIA**   Horreum Margi
Scardona   Drinus   Margus   Tabiata
Tragurium   Salonæ   Delminium   Ad. Matricem   **SUPERIOR**   Naiss
Brattia   Naro   AUTARITÆ   **M**
Pharia   **Narona**   M   **Dardania**
PLERÆI   M
Melite   Pardua   *Salluntum*
Epidaurus   **Pirustæ**
Rhizonicus Sinus   Riginium   Doclea   Ulpiana   Margus
(Rhizon)
42   Labeates L.   Scodra   Scardus M.   Scupi
Ulcinium   Axius   Bylazora
M A R E   Lissus   Stobi   Pæo
Drilon   **M A C E**
H A D R I A T I C U M   TAULANTII   Candavia M.
Dyrrhachium   Scampa   Lychnidus
(Epidamnus)   Pelagonia
Apollonia   Tomarus   Lyncestis   Ege
DESSARES   Begorrites   Edess
M A C E D O N I A   Byllis   Apsus   L.   Beroe
THRACIA, ILLYRICUM   Aulon   Eordæa
MŒSIA AND DACIA   Aous   **Orestis**   Italmon
40   *English Miles*   Elimea   Ob
0 20 40 60 80 100   **E P I R U S**

16   18   20   22

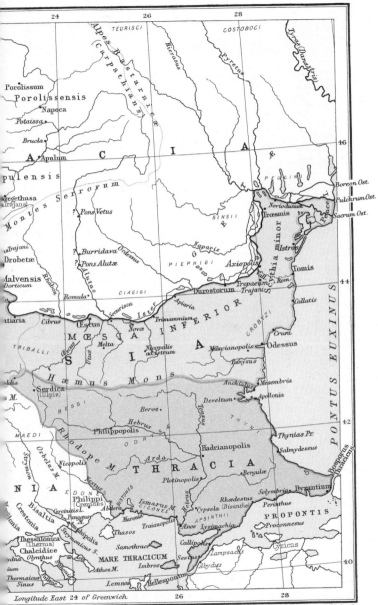

TEURISCI

COSTOBOGI

Alpes Bastarnicæ

Tyras (Danastris)

Porolissum

Porolissensis

Napoca

Potaissa

Brucla

A   Apulum

pulensis

Zegethusa
(Trajana)

Montes Serrorum

? Pons Vetus

? Burridava

Drobetæ

? Pons Alutæ

Malvensis

Dorticum

Romula

tiaria

Cibrus

TRIBALLI

ldia

M.

MAEDI

NIA

Strymon

Orbelus M.

Bisaltia

Crestonia

Thessalonica
(Therma)

Chalcidice

ydna   Olynthus

ium

Thermaicus

Sinus

Carpathians

Hierasus

Pyretus

SINSII

Naparis

PIEPHIGI

Ordessus

CIAGISI

Securisca

Oescus

Novæ

Melta

Trajani

Rhabon

Alutas

Ister

Apiaria

Trimammium

Nicopolis
ad Istrum

DACIA

PEUCINI

Noviodunum

Troesmis

Scythia Minor

Istros

Axiopolis

Rom.

Tropaeum
Trajani

Boreon Ost.

Pulchrum Ost.

Sacrum Ost.

Tomis

Callatis

Durostorum

MOESIA   INFERIOR

CROBYZI

Marcianopolis

Panysus

Crunæ

Odessus

Haemus   Mons

Serdica
(Ulpia)

BESSI

Beroe

Hebrus

Philippopolis

ODRYSAE

Arda

THRACIA

Nicopolis

Nestus

Rhodope M.

EDONES

Philippi
(Crenides)

Pangaeus M.

Crestonia   Amphipolis

Strymonicus S.

Symbolum

Thermaicus

Pallene   Acte

Anchialus

Develtum

Tonzus

THYNI

Mesembria

Apollonia

Hadrianopolis

Bergulæ

Plotinopolis

Arzus

Hebrus

Salmydessus

Thynias Pr.

Bosporus
Thracius

Byzantium

Selymbria

Rhædestus

Cypsela (Bisanthe)

BISTONES   Ismarus M.

Abdera   CICONES

Maronia

Cercinitis L.

Traianopolis

Thasos

Samothrace

Olynthus

Athos M.

MARE   THRACICUM

Imbros

Lemnos

Perinthus

Proconnesus

PROPONTIS

Cyzicus

Enos   Lysimachia

APSINTHII

Callipolis

Lampsacus

Sestus

Abydus

Hellespontus

PONTUS   EUXINUS

Longitude East 24 of Greenwich

© — John Bartholomew & Son. Ltd. Edinburgh

40

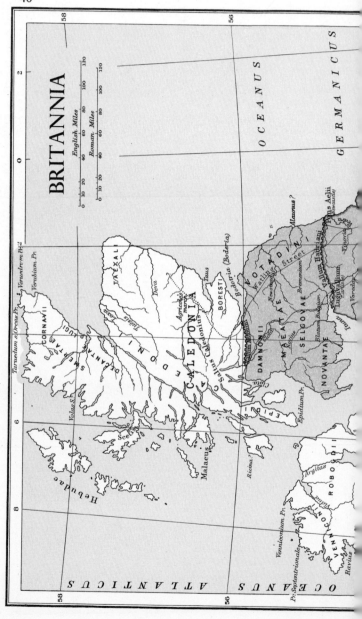

BRITANNIA

English Miles
0 10 20 40 60 80 100 120

Roman Miles
0 10 20 40 60 80 100 120

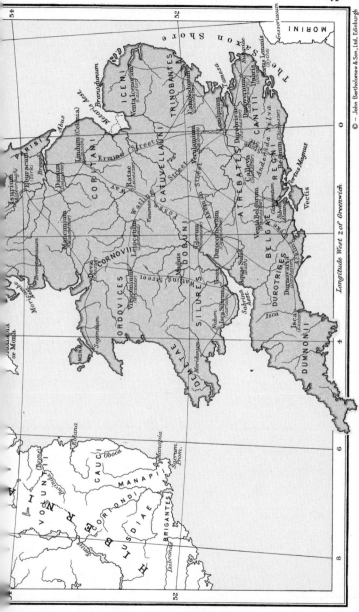

The Saxon Shore

MORINI

ICENI

TRINOBANTES

CANTII

ATREBATES

REGNI

BELGAE

DUROTRIGES

DUMNONII

CATUVELLAUNI

DOBUNI

CORITANI

CORNOVII

SILURES

ORDOVICES

DEMETAE

PARISI

BRIGANTES

HIBERNIA

VOLUNTII

DARINI

ROBOGDII

CAUCI

MANAPII

CORIONDI

USDIAE

Longitude West 2° of Greenwich

© – John Bartholomew & Son, Ltd., Edinburgh

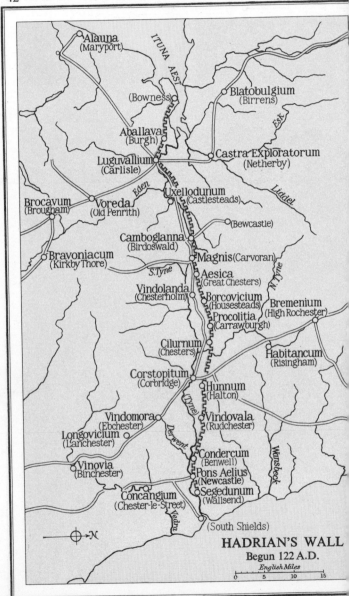

Alauna (Maryport)

ITUNA AEST

(Bowness)

Blatobulgium (Birrens)

Esk

Aballava (Burgh)

Luguvallium (Carlisle)

Castra Exploratorum (Netherby)

Eden

Uxellodunum (Castlesteads)

Liddel

Brocavum (Brougham)

Voreda (Old Penrith)

(Bewcastle)

Camboglanna (Birdoswald)

Magnis (Carvoran)

Bravoniacum (Kirkby Thore)

S. Tyne

Aesica (Great Chesters)

N. Tyne

Vindolanda (Chesterholm)

Borcovicium (Housesteads)

Procolitia (Carrawburgh)

Bremenium (High Rochester)

Cilurnum (Chesters)

Habitancum (Risingham)

Corstopitum (Corbridge)

Hunnum (Halton)

Tyne

Vindomora (Ebchester)

Derwent

Vindovala (Rudchester)

Longovicium (Lanchester)

Condercum (Benwell)

Pons Aelius (Newcastle)

Vinovia (Binchester)

Segedunum (Wallsend)

Wansbeck

Concangium (Chester-le-Street)

Vedra

(South Shields)

→N

HADRIAN'S WALL

Begun 122 A.D.

English Miles

0   5   10   15

© – John Bartholomew & Son, Ltd.

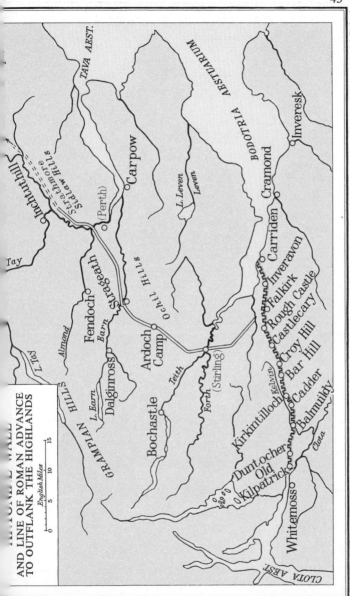

ANTONINE WALL
AND LINE OF ROMAN ADVANCE
TO OUTFLANK THE HIGHLANDS

English Miles
0 5 10 15

© – John Bartholomew & Son. Ltd. Edinburgh

Inchtuthill

TAVA AEST.

Strathmore

Sidlaw Hills

Carpow

(Perth)

Tay

L. Tod

Almond

Fendoch

Barn

Strageath

Dalginross

L. Barn

GRAMPIAN HILLS

Ardoch Camp

Bochastle

Ochil Hills

Teith

L. Leven

Leven

Forth

(Stirling)

BODOTRIA AESTUARIUM

Inveresk

Cramond

Carriden

Inveravon

Falkirk

Rough Castle

Castlecary

Croy Hill

Bar Hill

Cadder

Balmuildy

Kelvin

Kirkintilloch

Duntocher

Old Kilpatrick

Whitemoss

Clota

CLOTA AEST.

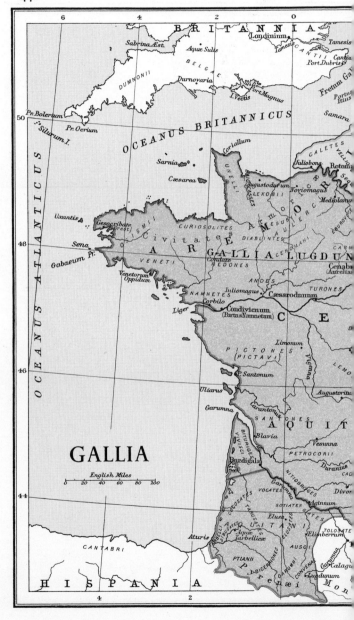

© – John Bartholomew & Son. Ltd. Edinburgh

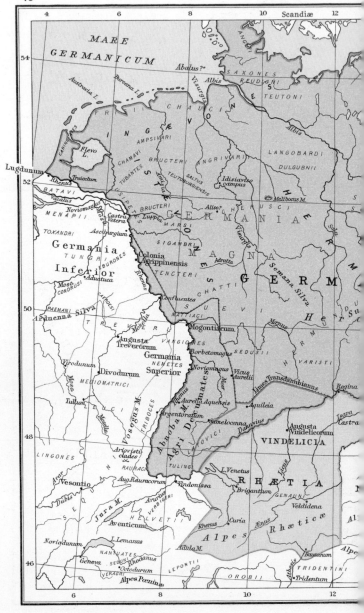

GERMANIA

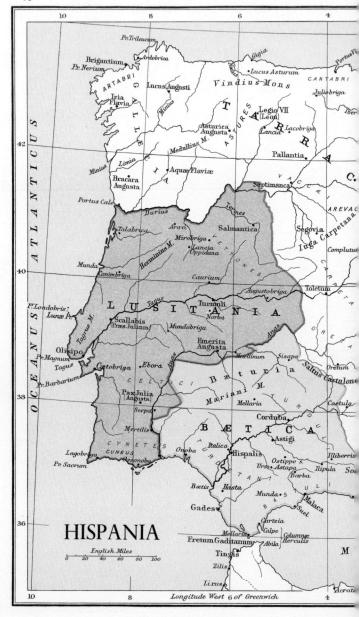

HISPANIA

English Miles
0   20   40   60   80   100

Longitude West 6 of Greenwich

© – John Bartholomew & Son, Ltd., Edinburgh

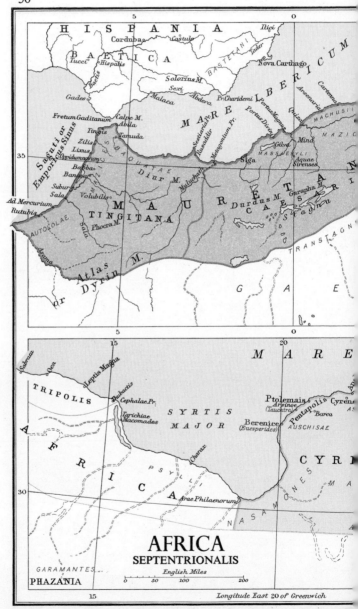

HISPANIA

5

0

Cordubas   Castulo
        Ilici
B AE TI C A
Tucci
Hispalis   Basterani   Tader
        Baetis   Nova Carthago
        Solorius M.   IBERICUM
Gades   Sexi   Abdera   Pr.Charidemi   Cartenna
        Malaca   Portus Magnus   Arsenaria
                    MACHUSII
Fretum Gaditanum Calpe M.   Quiza   MAZIC
        Abila   Scutariam   Rusaddir
Tingis   Tamuda   Metagonium Pr.   Gilva   Mina
Zilis   Siga   MASSAESYLI
35   Lixus   Malucha fl.   Aquae
    Oppidumnovum   Sirenses
Babba   Durdus M.   Garapha M.
Banasa   Diur M.   MAURE TA N
Suburba   CAESARI
Sala   Volubilis   M A   Saldae
                TINGITANA
Ad Mercurium   Phocra M.   TRANSTAGN
Rutubis
    AUTOLOLAE   Sala fl.
        Anatis   G   A   E
    Atlas
    or   Dyrin   M.

5   0

15   20
        M A R E   E
Sabrata
    Oea   Leptis Magna   Ptolemais   Cyrene
TRIPOLIS   Arsinoe   Pentapolis
    Neubactis   SYRTIS   (Tauchira)   Barca   AS
A   Cephalae Pr.   MAJOR   Berenice   AUSCHISAE
F   Tgrichiae   (Euesperides)
    Macomades
R   CYR
I   PSYLLI   Charax
C   MA
A   NASAMONES
30   A   Arae Philaenorum
                NASA
                    MONES

AFRICA
SEPTENTRIONALIS
English Miles
GARAMANTES   0   50   100   200
PHAZANIA

15   Longitude East 20 of Greenwich

MARE INTERNUM

Rusuccurru *Iomnium* *Rusucurru* *Iomnium* *Tigisis Pr.* *Tretum Pr.* *Igilgili* *Tucca*

Saldae

BYZIM. *Rusicade* *Chullu* *Tacatua* *Cappsa*

Hippo Regius

Utica
Thabraca
HIPPO Diarrhytus
Hippo-Apollinis
Pr. Apollinis
Membronis I.
CARTHAGO
Pr. Mercurii
Clupea
Cossyra I.

BANIURI M.
Auzia
Sitifis

Cirta
Ampsaga
Thagaste
Bulla Regia
Bordalis
Thuburbo
Tuni
Thignica
Simitthu
Thaca
Neapolis

MASSYLI
Naraggara
Madaura
Sicca
Veneria
Zama
Regia
Horrea Caelia
Hadrumetum
Leptis Minor
Thapsus

ZEUGITANA

Tingad
Lambaesa
Theveste
Thala
Sufes
Acholla
Brachodes Pr.

Sufetula
Thysdrus
Cercina I.

A
E
M
P
O
R
I
A
I
C
A

BYZACIUM

35

Aquae
Herculis
Aurasins M.
MUSULAMII
Thelepte
Thaenae

Bescera
Capsa
SYRTIS MINOR
Macomades

NUMIDIA
Ad Badias
Ad Maiores
Pallas Pr.
Tacape
I. Meninx

Libyca
Palus
Nepte
MAXYES
Trionis
Palus
Tauris
Tamalleni

Sabratha

MACHLYES
AUSEES

LOTOPHAGI

U
L
I

A

Cydamus

INTERNUM

25
30
M

GAMMAE
Panormus
Paraetonium
Catabathmus Minor
Phoenicus

Canopus
Nili Ostia

ICA
Catabathmus
Maior
ADYRMACHIDAE
ALEXANDRIA
Pharos
Mareotis P.
Buto
Oasis
Naucratis
Pelusinm

ARIDAE
Busiris
Bubastis
Athribis

LIBYA
DELTA
Heliopolis
30

Letopolis

Deserta Libyca
AEGYPTUS
Memphis
L. Moeris
Aphroditopolis

Ammonium
Oasis Minor
Oxyrynchus
Hipponon
Antinoe

Hermupolis

25
30

© – John Bartholomew & Son, Ltd., Edinburgh

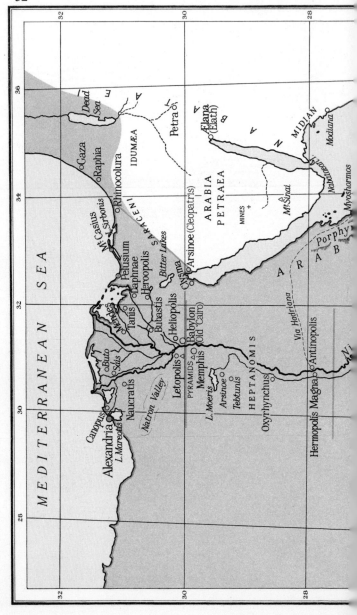

32

30

28

36

34

32

30

28

32

30

28

Dead Sea

E

IDUMÆA

Petra o

Elana (Elath)

MIDIAN

Modiana

oGaza

oRaphia

oRhinocolura

N

ARABIA PETRAEA

MINES +

Mt Sinai

Nabatæan

Myoshormos

Mt Casius

Sirbonis

SARACENI

Porphy

Pelusium

oDaphnae

Heroopolis

Bitter Lakes

Arsinoe (Cleopatris)

Mendes

oTanis

Bubastis

o Clysma

A R A B

Buto

oSais

Heliopolis

Babylon (Old Cairo)

M E D I T E R R A N E A N   S E A

Canopus

L. Mareotis

Alexandria

Naucratis

Natron Valley

Letopolis

PYRAMIDS △O

Memphis

L. Moeris

Arsinoe o

Tebtunis

HEPTANOMIS

Via Hadriana

oAntinopolis

Ni

Oxyrhynchus

Hermopolis Magna

N

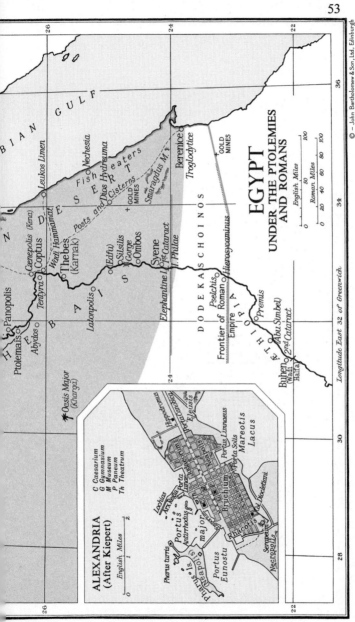

EGYPT
UNDER THE PTOLEMIES
AND ROMANS

English Miles
0   50   100
Roman Miles
0   20   40   60   80   100

© — John Bartholomew & Son, Ltd., Edinburgh

BIAN GULF

Leukos Limen

Nechesia

Fish Eaters

Dios Hydreuma

Posts and Cisterns

Berenice

GOLD MINES

Troglodytice

Smaragdus M.

GOLD MINES

Canepolis (Kena)

Coptus

Wadi Hammamat

Thebes (Karnak)

Panopolis

Tentyra

B A I S

Abydos

Ptolemais

Latonopolis

(Edfu)

Silsilis

Gorge

Ombos

Syene

Elephantine I.

1st Cataract

Philae

DODEKASCHOINOS

Pselchis

Frontier of Roman Empire

Hierosycaminus

Premis

A I T H I O P I A

Abu Simbel

Buhen

Wadi Halfa

2nd Cataract

Oasis Major (Kharga)

Longitude East 32 of Greenwich.

DESERT

N

E

ALEXANDRIA
(After Kiepert)

C Caesarium
G Gymnasium
M Museum
P Paneum
Th Theatrum

English Miles
0   1   2

Hippodromus

Porta Canopica

Eleusis

Portus Limnaeus

Mareotis Lacus

Necropolis

Nicopolis

Porta Solis

Bruchium

Porta Canobica

Rhacotis

Serapeum

Diocletiani

Lochias

Arx Rega

Portus Magnus

Portia Andriholtis

Pharus turris

Pharus Is.

Portus Eunostu

ASIA MINOR
AND SYRIA

English Miles

0 20 40 60 80 100 120 140

Longitude East 30 of Greenwich

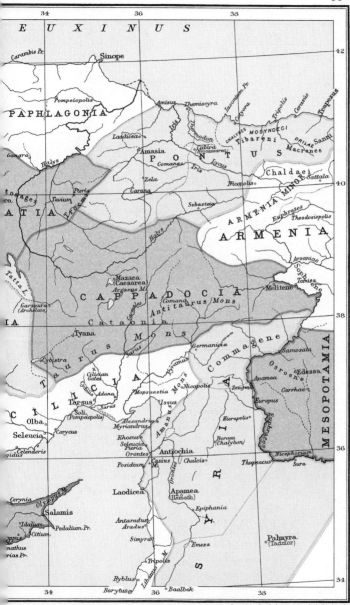

© – John Bartholomew & Son. Ltd. Edinburgh

56

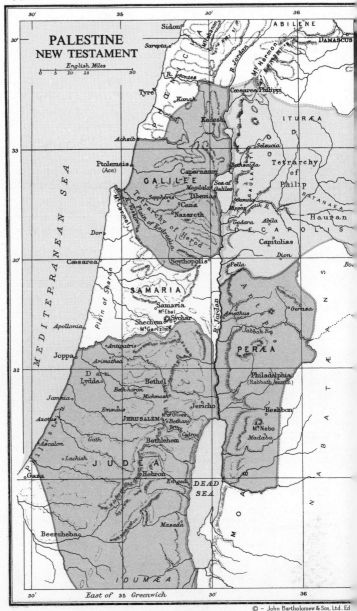

PALESTINE
NEW TESTAMENT

English Miles

© – John Bartholomew & Son, Ltd. Ed

INDEX
to the
CLASSICAL ATLAS

F

INDEX

to the

CLASSICAL ATLAS

It has been the tradition of this Atlas to give an index of places located by their latitude and longitude, in that order and in round figures, which are generally sufficient, sometimes with a word or two of description, to guide the eye to the right position on the map-page referred to. Among abbreviations often used are the obvious M. for Mons, Montes, or Mountain(s), I. for Insula(e) or Island(s), L. for Lacus or Lake. Pr. is for Promontorium or Cape, Aest. for Aestuarium or river-mouth, and, where space is precious on this size of map, we may be excused an occasional S. for Sinus or Gulf, Pal. for Palus or Paludes, marshes, or even Rm. for Regnum or Kingdom, where the context helps it out, as in India.

59

G

H

PHOTOGRAPHS

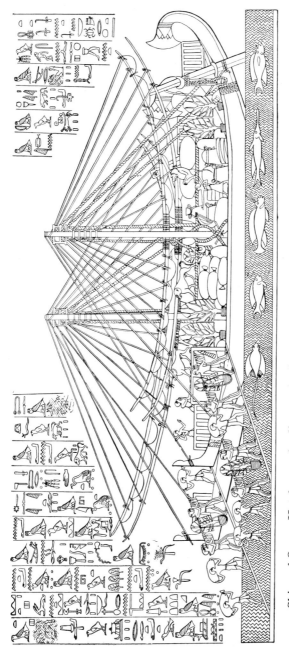

Ships of Queen Hatshepsut loading at the Incense Terraces of Punt, about 1500 B.C. (see p. xv)

Photo: E.N.A.

KARNAK

A bas-relief in the Great Temple, showing Seti I (*c.* 1300 B.C.) in his war chariot driving his Hittite enemies before him

Photo: British Museum

Babylonian map of the world

(see p. xviii)

Delphi

Temple of Apollo at Delphi

Photo: E.N.A.

Cup of Arcesilas II of Cyrene, about 550 B.C.
(see Thomson, *H.A.G.*, p. 67)

Photo: Mansell Collection

Greek temple at Poseidonia (Paestum) in southern Italy

Acragas (Agrigentum, now Girgenti)

Photo: E.N.A.

105

The Theatre at Epidaurus

Photo: Alinari

Athens, the Acropolis

Photo: Alinari

The Parthenon, Athens

The Agora, Athens, 1955, showing the Hephaestion (*background*) and the circular floor of Tholes (*left foreground*)

Photo: E.N.A.

Persepolis: an aerial view showing, on the right, the restored harem palace of Darius

Photo: E.N.A.

Persepolis: the broad double stairway to one of the two entrance halls near the royal palace of ... in the distance the ruins of the palace of Darius

Photo: Keystone Press

Lion-hunt mosaic recently found at Alexander's little capital, Pella

III

Coin of Graeco-Bactrian king with elephant's
scalp (see p. xxxiii)

Impression of Athena from the seal of an Indian
trader on the old Silk Road (see p. xxxix)

Photo: Mansell Collection

Forum Romanum: a general view from the Capitol

ARCH OF TITUS, ROME
The relief depicts
Roman soldiers carry-
ing off the table with
the spoils from the
Temple at Jerusalem

Roman aqueduct at Pont du Gard, Nîmes

A general view of Pompeii with Vesuvius in the distance

Child's labyrinth at Pompeii:
'hic habitat Minotaurus'

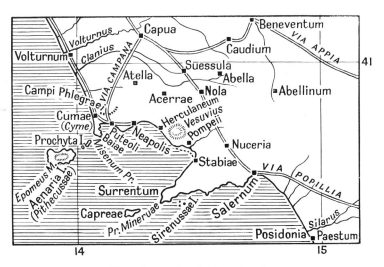

Vesuvius and neighbourhood

Photo: E.N.A.

Hadrian's Wall at Housesteads

Photo: E.N.A.

Hadrian's Wall

Photo: E.N.A.

Medina Medina Al-Arah. Arch of Trajan

Photo: Yenah, Tripoli

Sabrata (Libya): the theatre

Photo: Yenah, Tripoli

Leptis Magna (Libya): the theatre

Photo: E.N.A.

Palmyra: a general view, showing the Temple of the Sun

Photo: E.N.A.

Palmyra: a ruined street

Photo: Mansell Collection

Trajan's Column, celebrating his Dacian campaigns